STRATEGIC STUDIES INSTITUTE

The Strategic Studies Institute (SSI) is part of the U.S. Army War College and is the strategic-level study agent for issues related to national security and military strategy with emphasis on geostrategic analysis.

The mission of SSI is to use independent analysis to conduct strategic studies that develop policy recommendations on:

- Strategy, planning, and policy for joint and combined employment of military forces;

- Regional strategic appraisals;

- The nature of land warfare;

- Matters affecting the Army's future;

- The concepts, philosophy, and theory of strategy; and,

- Other issues of importance to the leadership of the Army.

Studies produced by civilian and military analysts concern topics having strategic implications for the Army, the Department of Defense, and the larger national security community.

In addition to its studies, SSI publishes special reports on topics of special or immediate interest. These include edited proceedings of conferences and topically oriented roundtables, expanded trip reports, and quick-reaction responses to senior Army leaders.

The Institute provides a valuable analytical capability within the Army to address strategic and other issues in support of Army participation in national security policy formulation.

The United States Army War College

The United States Army War College educates and develops leaders for service at the strategic level while advancing knowledge in the global application of Landpower.

The purpose of the United States Army War College is to produce graduates who are skilled critical thinkers and complex problem solvers. Concurrently, it is our duty to the U.S. Army to also act as a "think factory" for commanders and civilian leaders at the strategic level worldwide and routinely engage in discourse and debate concerning the role of ground forces in achieving national security objectives.

The Strategic Studies Institute publishes national security and strategic research and analysis to influence policy debate and bridge the gap between military and academia.

The Center for Strategic Leadership and Development contributes to the education of world class senior leaders, develops expert knowledge, and provides solutions to strategic Army issues affecting the national security community.

The Peacekeeping and Stability Operations Institute provides subject matter expertise, technical review, and writing expertise to agencies that develop stability operations concepts and doctrines.

The Senior Leader Development and Resiliency program supports the United States Army War College's lines of effort to educate strategic leaders and provide well-being education and support by developing self-awareness through leader feedback and leader resiliency.

The School of Strategic Landpower develops strategic leaders by providing a strong foundation of wisdom grounded in mastery of the profession of arms, and by serving as a crucible for educating future leaders in the analysis, evaluation, and refinement of professional expertise in war, strategy, operations, national security, resource management, and responsible command.

The U.S. Army Heritage and Education Center acquires, conserves, and exhibits historical materials for use to support the U.S. Army, educate an international audience, and honor Soldiers—past and present.

Strategic Studies Institute
and
U.S. Army War College Press

THE LIMITS OF OFFSHORE BALANCING

Hal Brands

September 2015

*****

Comments pertaining to this report are invited and should be forwarded to: Director, Strategic Studies Institute and U.S. Army War College Press, U.S. Army War College, 47 Ashburn Drive, Carlisle, PA 17013-5010.

*****

This manuscript was funded by the U.S. Army War College External Research Associates Program. Information on this program is available on our website, *www.StrategicStudies Institute.army.mil*, at the Opportunities tab.

*****

All Strategic Studies Institute (SSI) and U.S. Army War College (USAWC) Press publications may be downloaded free of charge from the SSI website. Hard copies of this report may also be obtained free of charge while supplies last by placing an order on the SSI website. SSI publications may be quoted or reprinted in part or in full with permission and appropriate credit given to the U.S. Army Strategic Studies Institute and U.S. Army War College Press, U.S. Army War College, Carlisle, PA. Contact SSI by visiting our website at the following address: *www.StrategicStudiesInstitute.army.mil.*

*****

The Strategic Studies Institute and U.S. Army War College Press publishes a monthly email newsletter to update the national security community on the research of our analysts, recent and forthcoming publications, and upcoming conferences sponsored by the Institute. Each newsletter also provides a strategic commentary by one of our research analysts. If you are interested in receiving this newsletter, please subscribe on the SSI website at *www.StrategicStudiesInstitute.army.mil/newsletter.*

ISBN 1-58487-702-2

FOREWORD

The United States is likely to face crucial grand strategic decisions in the coming years. This being the case, it is essential to have a rigorous, well-informed debate not simply about the nation's current grand strategy and policies, but about the most salient grand strategic options and alternatives open to the United States as well. In this monograph, Professor Hal Brands contributes to that debate through a probing analysis of one particular grand strategic alternative that has become increasingly prominent in recent years — the concept of "offshore balancing."

Offshore balancing entails a large-scale strategic retrenchment of America's current presence overseas, and it has often been touted by its supporters as a sort of grand strategic panacea — an option that will allow the United States to improve its overall geopolitical position while simultaneously slashing the costs of its global posture. As Professor Brands argues, however, these claims are misleading. The sort of large-scale strategic retrenchment envisioned according to offshore balancing would bring geopolitical and financial benefits that would likely be modest at best; it would also court risks and dangers that would probably be quite significant. Offshore balancing may seem attractive at first glance, but upon closer inspection, Professor Brands writes, there is much reason to question its desirability as a grand strategy for the United States.

The debate about America's current and future role in the world will undoubtedly continue in years to come, as analysts assess — and argue about — the merits and demerits of ideas like offshore balancing. The Strategic Studies Institute is pleased to offer this monograph as an important perspective in that debate.

Douglas C. Lovelace, Jr.

DOUGLAS C. LOVELACE, JR.
Director
Strategic Studies Institute and
    U.S. Army War College Press

ABOUT THE AUTHOR

HAL BRANDS is on the faculty at the Sanford School of Public Policy at Duke University. During 2015-16, he is also serving as a Council on Foreign Relations International Affairs Fellow in Washington, DC. Professor Brands is the author of three books, including *What Good is Grand Strategy? Power and Purpose in American Statecraft from Harry S. Truman to George W. Bush* (2014), and *Latin America's Cold War* (2010). He has also written numerous articles on grand strategy, U.S. foreign policy, and other international security issues. Professor Brands holds a Ph.D. in history from Yale University.

SUMMARY

Should the United States undertake a fundamental strategic retrenchment? Should it roll back, and perhaps do away with, the system of overseas security commitments and military deployments that have anchored its international posture since World War II? Many academic and strategic studies observers have answered "yes" to these questions in recent years. They assert that America's long-standing, postwar grand strategy has become both dispensable and self-defeating — dispensable because that grand strategy is no longer needed to sustain an advantageous global environment, and self-defeating because it wastes finite means while eliciting adverse behavior from allies and adversaries alike. The proper response to this situation, they believe, is to adopt a minimalist approach referred to as "offshore balancing." Briefly stated, offshore balancing envisions a dramatic reduction in America's overseas military deployments and alliance commitments, and a shift toward greater restraint and modesty in U.S. policy writ large. It is premised on the idea that this type of retrenchment will actually produce better security outcomes at a better price — that when it comes to grand strategy, less will actually be more.

Offshore balancing is thus a concept with growing currency and salience in the debate over the future of America's approach to international affairs. As this monograph argues, however, the case for offshore balancing is actually much weaker than it initially seems. Offshore balancing derives its appeal from the notion that it can produce the best of all worlds — improved geopolitical outcomes at reduced financial costs. Yet, as a more critical assessment makes clear, offshore balancing promises far more than it can plausibly deliver. The probable benefits of that strategy—both financial and geopolitical—are frequently exaggerated, while the likely disadvantages and dangers are far more severe than its proponents acknowledge. In essence, offshore balancing hinges on a series of shaky and often unpersuasive claims about what the world would look like subsequent to a major retraction of American power. Once those claims come under close scrutiny, the appeal of offshore balancing crumbles. In all likelihood, adopting this strategy would not allow the United States to achieve more security and influence at a lower price. The more plausible results would be to dissipate American influence, to court heightened insecurity and instability, and to expose the United States to greater long-range risks and costs.

THE LIMITS OF OFFSHORE BALANCING[1]

INTRODUCTION

Should the United States embrace a fundamentally more modest and circumscribed approach to world affairs? Is it time for Washington to roll back, and perhaps do away with, the vast system of overseas security commitments and forward military deployments that have anchored its international posture since World War II? An expanding group of academic and strategic studies observers have answered "yes" to these questions in recent years. They assert that America's long-standing, grand strategy has become both dispensable and self-defeating—dispensable because that grand strategy is no longer needed to secure U.S. interests and sustain an advantageous global environment, and self-defeating because it wastes finite means while eliciting adverse behavior from allies and adversaries alike. The proper response to this situation, they believe, is to adopt a minimalist approach usually referred to as "offshore balancing."[2] At its core, offshore balancing envisions a dramatic reduction in America's overseas military deployments and alliance commitments and a shift toward greater restraint in U.S. foreign policy writ large. It is based on the seemingly counterintuitive idea that this type of retrenchment actually will produce better security outcomes at a better price—that when it comes to grand strategy, less will actually be more.

"Less is more" is always a tempting proposition, and the attraction seems particularly strong of late. For at least a decade, offshore balancing has represented the preferred grand strategy for many international relations scholars of the realist persuasion,

1

including eminent analysts like Stephen Walt, John Mearsheimer, Barry Posen, and Christopher Layne. In the aftermath of the Iraq War and the global financial crisis of 2007-08, the overall visibility and popularity of the concept have increased further still. The appeal of offshore balancing has "jumped from the cloistered walls of academe to the real world of Washington policymaking," wrote one proponent of the concept in 2012; the case for a "dramatic strategic retrenchment" is gaining strength.[3] Offshore balancing, another leading scholar adds, represents "an idea whose time has come."[4]

Offshore balancing is indeed a concept with significant currency in the ongoing debate on the future of American grand strategy. Unfortunately, assessments of that concept have often been one-sided and incomplete. Because offshore balancing commands such strong backing within the academic strategic studies community, and because it is generally advanced as part of a critique of America's existing grand strategy, analysts have too rarely treated that proposal with the sort of sustained, in-depth scrutiny that is required to adequately judge both its advantages and its limitations.[5] The aim of this monograph is to redress that asymmetry through a critical assessment that explicates the core premises and rationale of offshore balancing in some detail, and then more vigorously probes its principal claims. The time is ripe for this sort of examination. The coming years will undoubtedly confront American officials with choices of great importance regarding U.S. global posture and policy. A more rigorous evaluation of prominent grand strategic ideas and alternatives is thus vital.[6]

The outcomes of such an evaluation cast serious doubt on the desirability, and even the basic viability, of offshore balancing. That strategy derives its attraction from the idea, as Walt has argued, that it will allow America to increase its national security and influence, while also decreasing "the resistance that its power sometimes provokes."[7] In reality, however, offshore balancing promises far more than it can deliver. The probable benefits of that approach — both financial and geopolitical — are frequently exaggerated, while the likely disadvantages and dangers are far more severe than its proponents acknowledge. Offshore balancing ultimately hinges on a series of shaky and often unpersuasive claims about what the world would look like subsequent to a major retraction of American power. Once those claims come under close scrutiny, the appeal of offshore balancing crumbles. In all likelihood, adopting this strategy would not allow the United States to achieve more security and influence at a lower price. The more plausible results would be to dissipate American influence, to court heightened insecurity and instability, and to expose the United States to greater long-range risks and costs.

The remainder of this monograph proceeds as follows. First, I briefly outline the basic parameters and rationale of the postwar (and now, post-Cold War) grand strategy that offshore balancers criticize. Second, I unpack the logic, claims, and purported benefits of offshore balancing itself. Third, and at greatest length, I critically scrutinize what effects a shift to offshore balancing would likely have for U.S. interests across a range of important issues. Fourth, and finally, I summarize the findings of this monograph and briefly discuss the implications for current debates on American grand strategy.

UNDERSTANDING U.S. GRAND STRATEGY

Since World War II, the United States has followed a highly engaged and proactive grand strategy for shaping the international order. The particular manifestations of that grand strategy have changed from year to year and presidential administration to presidential administration, of course, but the underlying aspirations have remained largely the same. American officials consistently have promoted an open and integrated world economy in which the United States and other countries can prosper. They have sought to foster a stable and peaceful international order in which democracy can survive and flourish. Not least of all, they have sought to maintain an advantageous geopolitical balance by preventing hostile actors from asserting hegemony over any of the three overseas regions (Europe, East Asia, and the Persian Gulf) that are of crucial economic or strategic value to America, and by locking in favorable configurations of power and influence within each of these regions.[8] These basic goals have oriented U.S. grand strategy for roughly 70 years, representing broad and enduring elements of continuity in American policy.

The effort to attain these objectives, in turn, has been anchored by what scholars have accurately called America's "most consequential strategic choice": its decision to make formal and informal security commitments in key overseas regions, and to give substance and credibility to those commitments through the forward deployment of American troops. In Europe and East Asia, these arrangements developed formally and fairly quickly after World War II, through the formation of the North Atlantic Treaty Organization (NATO) in the former region and a hub-

and-spokes network of bilateral alliances in the latter. Owing mainly to local political sensitivities and the residual British role "East of Suez," U.S. presence and commitments in the Persian Gulf generally developed later, more gradually, and more discreetly. Regional nuances notwithstanding, however, this willingness to assume a forward-leaning security posture in the core geopolitical zones of Eurasia has long served as the keystone of America's grand strategy.[9]

From the time of their creation, U.S. security commitments and force deployments were designed primarily to prevent any hostile power from dominating an area that was of fundamental importance to America's physical or economic security. Yet, these arrangements were equally meant to serve several other essential, interlocking purposes. American presence would submerge historical rivalries between members of the Western world, suppressing counterproductive security competitions, and enabling historically unprecedented cooperation on economic, political, and even military issues. That presence would also foster—in Europe and East Asia especially—the atmosphere of reassurance in which democracy and market-oriented economies could prosper. It would simultaneously slow the spread of nuclear weapons by easing the insecurity and instability that might otherwise encourage allies like Germany or Japan to develop independent nuclear arsenals. Finally, American forward presence would carry U.S. power deep into the most critical parts of the world, giving Washington an outsized capacity to impact regional affairs. In sum, forward deployments and security commitments would act as the linchpin of America's grand strategy, producing the influence, stability, and security necessary to accomplish a wide array of goals.[10]

It was a reflection of how enduring those goals were—and how much U.S. forward presence was seen to support them—that these arrangements largely remained in place even after the Cold War ended. As scholars like Melvyn Leffler have observed, the United States did not craft a wholly new grand strategy from scratch after the superpower struggle concluded.[11] It adapted its existing postwar grand strategy to the more advantageous circumstances of unipolarity. Washington reaffirmed its commitment to prevent any adversary from dominating a key region, to ensure that no country could command the resources and strategic position needed to challenge American primacy or American security. The United States also intensified its efforts to spread free markets and democracy overseas, and to contain those dangers—such as aggressive "rogue states" and nuclear proliferation—that might disrupt a very favorable post-Cold War order. Finally, and in support of all of these objectives, America kept large numbers of troops stationed abroad, while also maintaining—in some cases even expanding—its alliance commitments. In the unipolar era, as in the bipolar period preceding it, American officials averred, these commitments would foster the stability and influence needed to shape the international environment to Washington's benefit.[12]

Indeed, when viewed from a broad, 70-year perspective, America's postwar grand strategy can be said to have worked quite well. To be sure, the post-1945 record of U.S. policy contains no shortage of missteps and costly failures, from Vietnam to Iraq and beyond. But on the whole, America's highly engaged global posture generally has produced the desired results. It has facilitated, as various scholars have noted, the unprecedented international spread of democracy, and the establishment of a robust global market economy.[13] It has contributed to an extended period of great power peace, and to the containment of dangerous threats—whether regional or global—to international security and stability.[14] As recent research has shown, American strategy has also constituted a significant barrier to nuclear proliferation, by constraining the supply of critical components, and by simultaneously reassuring and dissuading countries that might otherwise have decided to go nuclear[15] and across all of these and other issues, U.S. alliance commitments and force deployments have played a vital enabling role. It is hardly surprising, then, that even as geopolitical circumstances have changed, the core components of American grand strategy—and especially the security commitments that have long served as its centerpiece—have remained enduring.

But for how long would those arrangements ultimately persist? Following the Cold War, some critics did start to question whether such a forward-leaning security posture was still essential or even desirable in a world that now lacked a hostile superpower adversary. "Come home, America," one prominent article declared; the time had come to seek "the disengagement of America's military forces from the rest of the world."[16] These concerns, and desires for geopolitical retrenchment more broadly, have grown far stronger of late. In recent years, the United States has been dealing with the fatigue and disillusion generated by its two inconclusive post-September 11, 2001 (9/11) wars, and the downward budgetary pressures generated by a brutal financial crisis and its aftermath. It has simultaneously been facing an international environment that seems to have become messier and more difficult than at any other time in a quarter-century.

These factors have all encouraged growing skepticism about the sustainability and wisdom of an assertive American globalism. In few quarters has that skepticism been more pronounced than among proponents of offshore balancing.

UNDERSTANDING OFFSHORE BALANCING

The multi-decade continuity in American grand strategy rests on recognition of that grand strategy's historical strengths. The case for offshore balancing, by contrast, proceeds from a sharp critique of the legacy grand strategy's apparent weaknesses.[17] Notwithstanding the overall postwar success of U.S. policy, offshore balancers tend to be highly dubious of the current value of America's long-standing approach to world affairs in general, and its existing system of alliances and force deployments in particular. In essence, they believe that, while these arrangements and the grand strategy they support were perhaps appropriate during the Cold War, they have become unnecessary, excessively expensive, and deeply counterproductive in the post-Cold War era.[18]

First and foremost, offshore balancers contend that the long-standing U.S. approach is unnecessary, because the geopolitical conditions that gave rise to America's postwar grand strategy have disappeared. U.S. security pledges and forward deployments were vital during the Cold War, they acknowledge, when Washington's allies were exposed and vulnerable, the Soviet Union was expansionist and menacing, and there was simply no other way of ensuring that vital strategic regions did not fall into enemy hands. In the post-Cold War period, however, the situation is very different. Many U.S. allies are wealthy, highly developed countries that have, or could easily field, powerful militaries. Because the international threat environment has become more benign with the absence of an aggressive global superpower, these countries can now be expected largely to provide for their own security and defense. There is very little short-term danger of a U.S. adversary dominating Europe or the Persian Gulf, offshore balancers point out, and even in the Asia-Pacific, China faces a number of proud and capable countries that would strongly contest any move toward regional hegemony. Thus, such vast U.S. commitments are no longer needed to ensure systemic stability; America's forward posture has become superfluous, a sort of "welfare for the rich."[19]

Not only superfluous, but profligate as well. Offshore balancers frequently point to the undeniably high costs of the legacy strategy, particularly annual defense budgets totaling over $500 billion (or even higher) in recent years. They argue that these costs strain American resources in ways that are unnecessary—given the post-Cold War dynamics noted earlier—and that will become progressively harder to manage amid leaner economic circumstances. "In coming years, the weakening of the U.S. economy and the nation's ballooning budget deficits are going to make it increasingly difficult to sustain the level of military commitments that U.S. hegemony requires," writes one scholar. Likewise, Barry Posen contends that "the Pentagon has come to depend on continuous infusions of cash simply to retain its current force structure—levels of spending that the United States' ballooning debt have rendered unsustainable."[20] This spendthrift approach, pro-retrenchment advocates allege, diverts resources from more pressing domestic priorities. Over the longer-term, it will further compromise American creditworthiness and deplete the fiscal and economic strength upon which national power ultimately depends.

Even in the nearer term, offshore balancers argue, current U.S. policies are deeply counterproductive because they elicit adverse reactions from both allies and adversaries. With respect to allies, America's posture can incentivize "reckless driving," in the sense that U.S. security commitments encourage friendly countries to take unwise geopolitical risks on the assumption that Washington will rescue them when things go bad. Perhaps more commonly, American guarantees and presence cause endemic free-riding or "cheap riding" because U.S. allies rationally calculate that they can underspend on defense as long as Washington is willing to overspend in order to protect them.[21] The majority of NATO allies spend below the Alliance's defense spending target of 2 percent of gross domestic product (GDP), while America generally devotes 3-4 percent of GDP to its military. The United States finds itself expending "increasingly precious funds on behalf of nations that are apparently unwilling to devote the necessary resources . . . to be serious and capable partners in their own defense," Secretary of Defense Robert Gates acknowledged in 2011.[22] An efficient strategy would get others to shoulder a larger burden so that America could bear a smaller one; the existing approach, offshore balancers allege, achieves the opposite result.

It also makes the United States less secure and influential by generating various forms of international pushback. Scholars like Robert Pape argue that excessive American power and activism have led to "soft balancing," as a wide range of countries, from allies to uncommitted nations to rivals, collaborate to constrain

U.S. action through diplomacy, international institutions, and other mechanisms.[23] Moreover, America's posture purportedly invites more dangerous reactions from both state and nonstate actors. According to Mearsheimer, for example, the post-Cold War expansion of NATO has served mainly to alienate Russia, eventually inviting the violent backlash seen in Georgia in 2008 and Ukraine since 2014.[24] In the same vein, Layne and other analysts argue that the U.S. presence in the Western Pacific unavoidably antagonizes China, which naturally sees that presence as a threat to its own ambitions and security. The result has been to encourage Beijing to build up its own capabilities, and to increase the prospect of sharp bilateral tensions, instability, and perhaps even war. "If the United States tries to maintain its current dominance in East Asia," Layne writes, "Sino-American conflict is virtually certain."[25] From this perspective, post-Cold War strategy has even had the effect of pushing potential U.S. rivals together, incentivizing Russia and China to pursue greater geopolitical cooperation in hopes of offsetting perceived encroachment by Washington.

For offshore balancers, the same counterproductive dynamic can be found in numerous other areas, as well. They argue, for instance, that it is precisely U.S. military presence in Muslim countries that provokes jihadist attacks: that the stationing of U.S. troops in Saudi Arabia from 1990 onward was a key cause of al-Qaeda's deadly campaign of terrorism against American targets, and that the occupation of Iraq after 2003 served as a principal incitement to extremist violence. Similarly, offshore balancers frequently argue that post-Cold War U.S. policy has encouraged rather than inhibited nuclear proliferation. By this logic, the combination of U.S. efforts to contain or even overthrow "rogue regimes" and the presence of American troops in close proximity to states like Iran and North Korea have exacerbated the feelings of insecurity that motivate nuclear proliferation in the first place. What current U.S. strategy misunderstands, three scholars write, "is that U.S. military hegemony is as likely to encourage nuclear proliferation, as states balance against us, as to prevent it."[26] In the eyes of offshore balancers, it is thus American strength, presence, and assertiveness that stimulate so many of the major threats that the country now faces.

Finally, offshore balancers believe that the long-standing strategy backfires because it leads to unwise and self-defeating uses of military force. During the Cold War, the thinking goes, the Soviet threat provided some discipline against capriciousness in the employment of American military power. Since then, however, any discipline has vanished, and simply possessing a globe-girdling military creates constant temptations to use that military even when vital interests are not at issue. "What's the point of having this superb military that you're always talking about if we can't use it?" Madeleine Albright once asked; for offshore balancers, the comment is indicative of a broader problem.[27] American leaders have become prone to seeking decisive military solutions to threats that could tolerably be contained or ignored; they use the Armed Forces in quixotic efforts to transform foreign societies and implant liberal institutions on decidedly inhospitable ground. The result is not to make America safer, but to draw the country into unending interventions that drain its resources and sow resentment and resistance abroad. Offshore balancers point to America's post-Cold War conflicts—most notably the invasion and occupation of Iraq—as proof of this lamentable tendency.[28]

To sum up, offshore balancers argue that the existing U.S. grand strategy has outlived its geopolitical utility, that it imposes unnecessary and unsustainable costs on the nation, and that it fosters blowback and overextension rather than security. The best way to correct these problems, they contend, is to embrace a very different approach to world affairs.

Offshore balancing is, at its core, a fairly straightforward concept. It derives directly from the realist tradition in international-relations scholarship, and so focuses heavily — almost entirely — on "system maintenance" and the preservation of an acceptable balance of power. In particular, offshore balancers believe that outside of the Western Hemisphere, there are three primary overseas regions — Europe, East Asia, and the Persian Gulf — that are of fundamental importance to U.S. interests because of the resources, wealth, and geopolitical geography that they command. Were one or more of these regions to come under control of an American adversary, that adversary might be able to generate the strength necessary to endanger the United States itself or to interfere massively and unacceptably with U.S. economic wellbeing. Offshore balancers therefore strongly affirm a core tenet of postwar U.S. statecraft — that the essential and overriding goal of American grand strategy must be to ensure that none of these regions are dominated by a hostile power.

Where offshore balancers depart from the legacy grand strategy is in their belief that permanent U.S. presence and alliance guarantees are neither necessary nor suitable to achieving this goal. Rather, offshore balancers argue that under normal circumstances the United States should depend on local actors to counter any threats that may emerge in the key regions, fortifying those local actors via political, economic, or indirect military support (such as arms sales) where necessary to maintain the balance. Only when an important regional equilibrium collapses or is in danger of collapsing—in other words, only when a hostile actor is set to conquer or otherwise dominate the area—should American military forces go "onshore" to intervene. Once the aggressor has been turned back and the balance repaired, U.S. forces should once again retreat offshore.[29]

It is therefore wrong to describe offshore balancing as an isolationist strategy, because its supporters firmly believe that Washington does have an essential interest in maintaining acceptable balances of power in important overseas regions. Instead, offshore balancing is properly seen as a minimalist, or free-hand strategy, because it asserts that America can attain that goal while also shedding obligations and resources.[30] Indeed, even though proponents of offshore balancing occasionally disagree when it comes to specific policy issues, they universally concur that their strategy involves a significant rolling back of permanent U.S. commitments and presence abroad. Washington should quit NATO's military command and perhaps withdraw from the Alliance itself, for example, or, at a bare minimum, it should terminate the peacetime American troop presence in Europe. The United States should likewise refuse any onshore peacetime presence in the Persian Gulf (and the Middle East more broadly), and rely solely on forces stationed "over the horizon" in the event of a severe crisis in the region. The situation is somewhat more complicated in East Asia, where most offshore balancers support maintenance of significant naval and air forces as a hedge against an ascendant China. Yet these scholars also propose, variously, removing U.S. troops from South

Korea, terminating the ambiguous U.S. commitment to defend Taiwan, revising or potentially ending the long-standing alliance with Japan, and withdrawing most or perhaps even all American forces from that country. This global military retrenchment, in turn, would be accompanied by a shift to a leaner force structure, involving drastic cuts in overall U.S. ground forces, and lesser but still deep cuts to the Navy and Air Force. In sum, offshore balancing calls for a far more austere U.S. security posture.[31]

It likewise envisions a more modest, realpolitik style in foreign relations more broadly. Precisely because offshore balancers are so heavily influenced by a realist tradition that purports to place cold, balance-of-power considerations above all else, they believe that the United States should unapologetically deprioritize issues and relationships that are not deemed essential to this bedrock concern. Washington should not seek "ideological" ends like the advancement of human rights or democracy — even by purely diplomatic means — if doing so requires jeopardizing relations with authoritarian countries that could otherwise be useful partners in preserving acceptable regional balances. "International politics is a contact sport," writes Walt, "and even powerful states cannot afford to be overly choosy when selecting allies and partners."[32] Likewise, U.S. policymakers should not maintain such close relationships with countries — such as Israel — that have long-standing ties of affection with America, but that offshore balancers now view as more of a strategic liability than an asset.[33] Nor, for that matter, should the United States seek to prevent nations like Russia or China from obtaining reasonably delimited spheres of influence within their regions — by asserting dominance over Ukraine or

Taiwan, for instance—so long as this expansion does not critically imperil the overall balance of power within those regions.[34]

Finally, and not least of all, offshore balancers believe that the United States must scrupulously refrain from any large-scale use of military force that is not intimately related to the central mission of preserving systematic balance and stability. This means generally foreswearing humanitarian intervention, or the use of force to promote or restore democracy overseas. It also means refraining from preemptive or preventive wars to combat weapons of mass destruction (WMD) proliferation, or to topple regimes that are internally noxious but could nonetheless be contained without resorting to large-scale conflict. With respect to terrorism, offshore balancers do normally approve of the use of force in dealing with the most dangerous and direct threats. But they strongly favor "light footprint" approaches featuring tools like drones and special forces, and they strongly oppose turning such interventions into the sort of prolonged counterinsurgency, nation-building endeavors undertaken in Iraq and Afghanistan. These and other "wars of choice" represent costly diversions from the core grand strategic preoccupation of managing the global configuration of power, offshore balancers argue; Washington must therefore pair retrenchment from its existing alliances and forward troop presence with a broader shift toward geopolitical modesty.[35]

There is little doubt, then, that offshore balancing would represent a significant rupture with the postwar and now post-Cold War template for U.S. strategy, and a retreat from the overall level of assertiveness and activism that have long marked American policy. Yet it is important to understand that offshore balancing would not be something entirely new for the United States. As Mearsheimer has written, the nation essentially practiced offshore balancing between 1898 and 1945, when it abstained from significant peacetime commitments in Europe and East Asia but eventually sent its forces into combat to prevent (or reverse) the domination of those regions by aggressive authoritarian powers in World Wars I and II.[36] More recently, American policy in the Persian Gulf prior to 1990 followed a roughly similar approach, with the United States depending first on local powers to maintain a regional equilibrium, and then bringing its own military capabilities to bear when Saddam Hussein's invasion of Kuwait broke that balance.[37] Proponents of offshore balancing thus contend that their preferred strategy is not really anything new. Rather, it represents a tried-and-true concept that America should once more embrace.

What specific benefits would such a shift bring? Advocates of offshore balancing advertise four major advantages. First, and most broadly, a move toward offshore balancing would purportedly enhance America's long-run global position by putting its strategic posture on a more sustainable foundation. Washington's existing grand strategy is itself unstable and self-defeating, offshore balancers claim, because it forces the United States to bear disproportionate burdens and runs counter to the ongoing diffusion of global power. The value of offshore balancing, by contrast, is that it would use that diffusion of power to American advantage. No more would the United States permit rich and capable allies to free-ride on its own taxing exertions. Quite the contrary—rolling back U.S. presence in key areas like Europe, East Asia, and the Persian Gulf would compel important regional players,

17

from Japan to Saudi Arabia to Germany, to assume a greater role in providing for their own security and that of the regions they inhabit. In effect, the strategy would employ the built-in balancing mechanisms within international relations — the natural tendency of states to do what is necessary to protect their own independence and well-being — to sustain a stable and advantageous global environment, while also distributing the responsibility for preserving that environment more proportionately. "Offshore balancing is a grand strategy based on burden shifting, not burden sharing," Christopher Layne writes. "It would transfer to others the task of maintaining regional power balances; checking the rise of potential global and regional hegemons; and stabilizing Europe, East Asia, and the Persian Gulf/Middle East."[38]

Burden shifting, in turn, would facilitate a second key benefit: markedly reduced costs for the United States. Almost by definition, offshore balancing would liberate America from the costs of military conflicts like the invasion and occupation of Iraq, prolonged stabilization operations in Afghanistan, and other such "discretionary" interventions that offshore balancers rule out *a priori*. More significantly, offshore balancers claim that the strategy would pay broader and longer-lasting financial dividends by permitting a shift to a trimmed-down force structure. Barry Posen predicts that a more restrained approach would allow the United States to slash its ground forces by half, and cut both the Navy and Air Force by between one-quarter and one-third, respectively. Likewise, Cato Institute scholar Christopher Preble estimates that this type of strategy would enable major reductions in the number of carrier strike groups, naval vessels, tactical fighter wings, and other high-dollar items, to say nothing of the savings that would come from sharp cuts in U.S. ground forces. The overall upshot would be to make U.S. strategy more economically viable, and to enhance the country's prospects for sustained prosperity and balanced budgets.[39]

Third, offshore balancers believe that this retrenchment would, in fact, improve America's ability to address the most pressing security challenges it currently faces. In great power relations, many offshore balancers believe that paring back America's security presence would make U.S. power appear far less menacing to regional powers like Russia and China, and decrease the impetus toward conflict with those countries.[40] In the event that a sharper confrontation with a challenger like China ensued anyway, a shift to offshore balancing would still benefit the United States by allowing it to avoid costly diversions elsewhere and to elicit greater contributions from other friendly countries in the area.[41] From this perspective, behaving with greater moderation and restraint would allow Washington to position itself far more advantageously in global strategic affairs.

The results would be similarly beneficial in other areas. Offshore balancers are virtually unanimous in positing that an end to U.S. forward presence and long-term troop deployments in the Middle East would undercut a primary source of Muslim anger toward America, and significantly defuse the threat of jihadist terrorism. Some extremist violence might still occur, Robert Pape allows, but offshore balancing remains "the best way to secure our interest in the world's key oil-producing region without provoking more terrorism."[42] Pressures for nuclear proliferation would also be greatly reduced in an offshore balancing scenario. Because offshore balancers assert that it is U.S. power, activism, and presence that largely push countries like North Korea and Iran to pursue nuclear weapons, they also assert that retrenchment would attack the underlying causes of rogue state proliferation. Pyongyang and Tehran would have less fear for the survival of their regimes; they would, accordingly, have less need for the ultimate weapon.[43] Across a whole array of vital issues — great power relations, nuclear proliferation, and terrorism — pulling back would thus make the United States more secure and effective by easing the pushback that its own policies have generated.

All of these advantages, in turn, relate closely to a fourth and final advertised benefit of offshore balancing, which is that it would actually make the United States more influential in world affairs. By decreasing unnecessary commitments and compelling others to shoulder greater burdens, offshore balancers believe, Washington would increase its flexibility and maximize its capacity to have decisive impact on those core geopolitical issues that really matter. By defusing the myriad forms of resentment and resistance that the current grand strategy allegedly causes, the United States would simultaneously undercut the pushback that corrodes its authority and efficacy. Finally, by playing "hard to get" with friends and allies — by allowing them to take less for granted, and forcing them to work harder to obtain American support — the United States could perhaps elicit higher levels of cooperation with its international agenda. Retrenchment, in all of these respects, would have the counterintuitive outcome of giving the United States additional leverage in the global arena.[44]

Indeed, if the arguments of its proponents are accepted as truth, then offshore balancing appears to be a nearly ideal strategic concept for America. It seems to offer the best of everything, promising enhanced security and influence, and an improved long-term strategic position, at a significantly reduced price. What remains, then, is to question whether the underlying logic and claims of offshore balancing can really bear close scrutiny. The disappointing but inescapable answer is that they mostly cannot.

ASSESSING OFFSHORE BALANCING: OVERSOLD BENEFITS, UNDERSTATED COSTS AND RISKS

The previous section presented the case for offshore balancing, by outlining its basic content, rationale, and expected benefits. This section subjects offshore balancing to a more critical assessment, by examining the probable advantages and disadvantages were that strategy actually adopted. As this analysis makes clear, the case for offshore balancing is far weaker than its proponents claim. The likely benefits—both financial and geopolitical—of that strategy are much less impressive than they first seem, while the risks and liabilities are potentially quite daunting.

What Savings?

Consider, first, the question of financial cost. One purported advantage of offshore balancing is that it will permit significant reductions in defense spending, and put U.S. strategy—and the country as a whole—on far better fiscal footing. "We spend too much," Christopher Preble argues, especially "relative to alternative strategies that will keep us safe, but at far less cost."[45] There would indeed be some economies if the United States were to adopt an offshore balancing type approach. The country would undoubtedly save some money if it simply refused to use military force in any circumstance in which a regional balance was not in imminent danger of collapsing (although whether this would be a sensible policy to follow is another matter.)[46] Moreover, an offshore balancing type military could probably be somewhat smaller and less costly than the current force, and it would presumably require far fewer overseas bases. There remain serious questions about **how much** smaller and cheaper that force would actually be, however, and there are important reasons to doubt that offshore balancing would really yield such significant financial dividends.

One such reason is that the legacy grand strategy—the baseline against which offshore balancing is either implicitly or explicitly compared—is in reality much less expensive than is often thought. To be sure, defense budgets that routinely exceed $500 billion annually consume massive amounts of money in absolute terms.[47] But when viewed in relative terms—as a percentage of GDP—U.S. military spending has actually been comparatively low since the Cold War. At the peak of that conflict during the 1950s, for instance, the United States regularly spent upward of 10 percent of GDP on defense, reaching 14.2 percent in 1953. Even in the 1980s, the figure was often upward of 6 percent.[48] Since the mid-1990s, however, total U.S. defense spending—including funds for overseas contingency operations like the wars in Iraq and Afghanistan—has generally been between 3 and 4 percent of GDP. It rose as high as 4.7 percent at the peak of U.S. deployments in Iraq and Afghanistan in 2010, but then dropped back under 4 percent in 2013 and has continued downward since then.[49] By relevant post-World War II standards, the United States has devoted a comparatively small percentage of its wealth to defense in the past 20 years, indicating that the costs of American presence and policy are not nearly as staggering as is sometimes claimed.

It is worth emphasizing that this holds true even when the cost of recent U.S. wars is considered. The wars in Iraq and Afghanistan were by far the costliest U.S. conflicts of the post-Cold War era, with operations and other war-related activities in those countries costing roughly $1.5 trillion between 2001 and 2014.[50] Nonetheless, the vast majority (well over 90 percent) of those costs are included in the figures cited in the preceding paragraph, meaning that, even during a period of manpower-intensive ground operations, U.S. defense costs were actually quite modest in historical context. This does not necessarily mean that the money spent in Iraq and Afghanistan was a productive investment, of course, but it does put the price tag of those conflicts in perspective. Moreover, given that these conflicts were actually massive outliers among America's post-Cold War interventions in terms of financial costs — and that the response to those costs has already been explicitly to downgrade the role of manpower-intensive stability operations in U.S. defense strategy — one begins to question whether a United States that remains globally engaged and present must necessarily incur the expenses associated with major Middle Eastern land wars on a regular basis.[51]

If the current grand strategy is not as expensive as it sometimes seems, then neither is offshore balancing as cheap as one might expect. The basic reason for this is that a military that can actually carry out an offshore balancing approach must still be capable of intervening quickly and decisively in regional contingencies, and forcing its way back onshore if a regional balance collapses. Despite its emphasis on retrenchment, Evan Braden Montgomery has recently observed, offshore balancing still hinges on the idea that "U.S. military power will remain sufficient to prevent any nation from dominating its neighbors through aggression or coercion."[52] An offshore balancing type military would have to possess the aerial and naval dominance necessary to command the global commons and provide access into contested theaters in time of conflict. This, presumably, would mean major continuing investments in the big-ticket, high-technology capabilities needed to maintain such an edge. That military would also have to possess—or very rapidly be able to generate—the ground forces needed to intervene successfully if a regional equilibrium began to slip away. In short, an offshore balancing type military would still need to be very ready and very powerful, capable of prompt, effective global power projection with all its massive expense. "While day-to-day demands on the U.S. military would be less in offshore balancing than in [a strategy of forward presence]," one informed analyst writes, "it is not clear whether total military requirements would be less burdensome."[53]

Could such a military still save considerable sums by closing overseas bases and stationing its forces within the United States? Not as readily as one might think. Because foreign countries often offset some costs of U.S. presence, and for other financial and logistical reasons, relocating American forces in this manner achieves only very meager reductions in expenditures. As one analysis by the RAND Corporation has noted, stationing two squadrons of F-16s in the United States instead of in Italy would result in savings of only 6 percent annually. Similarly, the Congressional Budget Office has estimated that returning nearly all overseas Army forces to the United States would yield annual savings of less than $1.5 billion. "At the level of grand strategy," the RAND study concludes, "the cost differences between CONUS [continental United States] and OCONUS [overseas] presence are insignificant."[54]

The same goes for America's nuclear arsenal. Partisans of offshore balancing have often argued that their strategy would permit major cuts in U.S. nuclear forces. Here too, however, the practical requirements of a sufficiently resourced offshore balancing approach are likely to be far more onerous than advertised. Even in an offshore balancing scenario, the United States would require a very robust nuclear arsenal if it hoped to sustain extended deterrence as its overseas conventional force posture was dramatically reduced. For if, as the Barack Obama administration noted in its 2010 *Nuclear Posture Review*, "strengthening the non-nuclear elements of regional security architectures is vital" to achieving further reductions in the U.S. nuclear arsenal, then weakening those non-nuclear elements via American retrenchment would logically place a higher premium on nuclear weapons.[55] Under an offshore balancing approach, superior nuclear forces would also be needed to ensure the escalation dominance that would allow the United States to intervene in regional crises without danger of being blackmailed or coerced by a powerful, nuclear-armed rival.[56] Consequently, offshore balancing would probably not permit significant reductions in the U.S. nuclear arsenal. Rather, it would entail the major—and very expensive—investments needed to modernize that arsenal in the coming years and decades.[57]

When these issues are factored into the equation, the financial benefits of offshore balancing seem considerably less striking. One scholar has projected that a strategy approximating offshore balancing could be sustained through military spending amounting to roughly 2.5 percent of U.S. GDP.[58] There are serious questions regarding whether the resulting military — which would possess substantially diminished naval, air, ground, and nuclear forces — would indeed be sufficient to accomplish the aforementioned tasks without courting intolerable risks of mission failure.[59] But even setting those questions aside for the sake of argument, this level of spending is only 0.5 percent of GDP lower than what the United States paid for defense in the late-1990s, and perhaps 1 percent of GDP lower than what military spending is projected to be in the near future.[60] Stated differently, even if one assumes that a force costing 2.5 percent of GDP could accomplish its stated objectives in an offshore balancing scenario, a shift to that strategy would result in defense-related savings of perhaps 16 to 29 percent relative to the relevant post-Cold War figures.

Such savings are certainly not trivial. If fully realized, they might reduce federal deficits that have ranged from nearly $500 billion to just over $1.4 trillion per year in the years since 2009 by perhaps $100-200 billion annually. But even in the most favorable scenario, these savings would still be much less than what is needed to balance the federal budget. In fact, because defense spending accounts for roughly 18 percent (and falling) of federal spending, and because present and out-year deficits are caused primarily by spiraling entitlement costs (48 percent and rising quickly as of 2014), the defense cuts that would accompany offshore balancing would have only a fairly marginal effect on the country's long-run fiscal prospects.[61] To put it another way, if the United States effectively addresses the ballooning cost of entitlements, it will easily be able to afford its current grand strategy well into the future. If it does not do so, then even far more draconian defense cuts will not close the fiscal gap.

Finally, it is reasonable to inquire whether offshore balancing might simply exchange these relatively modest short-term economies for higher long-term costs and burdens. Offshore balancing is premised on the notion that regional balances are inherently robust, and so the most expensive and dangerous types of military intervention will be quite rare. Yet an inconvenient truth for offshore balancers is that in each of the major cases in which America relied on that strategy during the past 100 years — in Europe and East Asia in the period of the world wars, and in the Persian Gulf in the period before 1990 — it ended up having to wage a major, high-intensity conflict to repair a regional equilibrium that had either broken entirely or was in imminent danger of breaking. In each of these instances, the United States eventually did beat back the offending aggressor and restore a favorable configuration of power, and so these episodes are generally treated as "successes" by offshore balancers. Yet, from a long-term perspective, perhaps the wiser and more economical choice would have been to accept the peacetime commitments that might have sustained the balance and prevented the situation from reaching such a critical and costly juncture. In Europe and East Asia especially, it was precisely this hard-earned awareness that foreswearing onshore commitments was a penny-wise but pound-foolish approach that caused the United States to embrace a much different strategy from 1945 onward. Many years have passed since then, but the basic truth remains the same: the financial argument for offshore balancing is weaker than it might initially appear.

Exaggerated Security Benefits: Terrorism.

The prospect of financial savings, of course, is but one aspect of offshore balancing's appeal. Its proponents also claim that the strategy will yield important security benefits by reducing the severity of critical threats like international terrorism and nuclear proliferation, and better positioning the United States to deal with those issues. If these claims were true, they would provide powerful vindication for offshore balancing and its "less can be more" ethos. In reality, however, the advantages of retrenchment are frequently inflated when it comes to these matters, while substantial dangers and drawbacks are often obscured or ignored.

This is certainly true with respect to terrorism. In fairness, offshore balancers certainly have a point in arguing that America's onshore presence in the Gulf and the larger Middle East has long served as a key source of incitement to jihadist attacks. It was U.S. intervention in Lebanon in 1982-84 that first brought America into the crosshairs of suicide terrorism by provoking Hezbollah's deadly bombings of the U.S. Embassy and Marine barracks in Beirut. In the Gulf specifically, the presence of U.S. troops in Saudi Arabia during and after the Persian Gulf Crisis of 1990-91 was indeed a primary motivator of al-Qaeda's escalating campaign of terrorism against American targets, and the later invasion and occupation of Iraq breathed new life into a jihadist movement that had been badly damaged in the wake of 9/11. The Iraq War, National Intelligence Council Chairman Robert Hutchings commented in 2005, acted as "a magnet for international terrorist activity" and a key recruiting device for al-Qaeda.[62] Finally, and at a broader level of analysis, scholarly research indicates that resentment of foreign troop deployments and military occupations have traditionally been leading causes of suicide terrorism.[63] There is thus little doubt that certain U.S. policies have fanned the flames of terror, as offshore balancers allege. More problematic, however, is the assertion that their preferred strategy would significantly reduce the threat.

One key reason for skepticism is that the military withdrawal that most offshore balancers envision is not the withdrawal that jihadist groups have demanded as the price of peace. When al-Qaeda and other groups call for a U.S. military withdrawal from the Muslim world, they are calling for the removal not simply of large-scale ground forces and other sizable units (the assets that most offshore balancers focus on in advocating retrenchment). Rather, they are calling for the removal of all forms of American military power and influence, including trainers and advisers, drones, security assistance and weapons sales, and other tools that would presumably continue to be crucial to counterterrorism, even in an offshore balancing context. "Even U.S. intelligence liaison, which involves sharing information, training, and other forms of exchange, is . . . a sensitive issue" for al-Qaeda and other jihadists, one expert writes.[64] This leaves advocates of retrenchment stuck with an awkward dilemma. Undertaking the truly comprehensive military withdrawal that al-Qaeda and other extremist groups demand would utterly cripple America's approach to counterterrorism as well as its broader ability to support friendly regimes in the region. Undertaking a lesser withdrawal, by contrast, might still assuage some anti-U.S. resentment, but it would presumably not mollify jihadist grievances to the extent that off-shore balancers believe.

This first reason for skepticism is reinforced by a second, which is that even though the deployment of American troops on Muslim lands has historical-ly been a cause of anti-U.S. extremism, it has never been the sole cause. That extremism also originated from grievances fueled by U.S. policy toward Iraq in the 1990s, long-standing American support for dicta-torial Arab regimes, the extensive and intimate U.S. relationship with Israel, and the perceived invasion of Muslim societies by Western cultural and economic influences. Many of these grievances were featured in early al-Qaeda pronouncements, including bin Lad-en's famous 1998 *fatwa* declaring that "the ruling to kill the Americans and their allies . . . is an individual duty for every Muslim who can do it."[65] Many of the same issues continue to figure prominently today. As al-Qaeda spokesman Adam Gadahn declared in 2010, removal of U.S. troops from the Persian Gulf and be-yond was only one of a series of requirements that Washington must meet in order to earn a respite from jihadist attacks:

> First, you must pull every last one of your soldiers, spies, security advisors, trainers, attaches, contrac-tors, robots, drones, and all other American person-nel, ships, and aircraft out of every Muslim land from Afghanistan to Zanzibar.

> Second, you must end all support—both moral and material—to Israel and bar your citizens from travel-

ing to Occupied Palestine or settling there, and you must impose a blanket ban on American trade with the Zionist regime and investment in it.

Third, you must stop all support and aid—be it military, political, or economic, or otherwise—to the hated regimes of the Muslim world. This includes the so-called "development aid" . . .

Fourth, you must cease all interference in the religion, society, politics, economy, and government of the Islamic world.

Fifth, you must also put an end to all forms of American and American-sponsored interference in the educational curricula and information media of the Muslim world.

And sixth, you must free all Muslim captives from your prisons, detention facilities, and concentration camps, regardless of whether they have been recipients of what you call a 'fair' trial or not.

"Your refusal to release our prisoners or your failure to meet any of our other legitimate demands," the pronouncement concluded, "will mean the continuation of our just struggle against your tyranny." As this statement indicates, anti-American terrorism has complex and multi-faceted causes, and foreswearing forward military presence in the Middle East would satisfy just one of a wide range of grievances.[66]

By truly adopting offshore balancing, in fact, Washington would merely inflame some of those grievances all the more. A strategy that ruled out stationing American forces in the region would unavoidably make the United States more dependent on its authoritarian Arab allies—Egypt, Jordan, Saudi Arabia, the smaller Gulf sheikdoms—as providers of security and stability. During the 1970s, for instance, America poured arms into the Persian Gulf autocracies, particularly Saudi Arabia and the Shah's Iran, at a time when it had only a skeletal military presence of its own in the area.[67] Retrenchment today would similarly imply increased American military sales, intelligence cooperation, and other forms of support for local allies, and a general accentuation of the "friendly dictators" approach that has so incensed Muslim radicals. By the same token, even though many advocates of offshore balancing argue that Washington should sharply curtail its security ties to Israel, commentators like Marc Lynch and Colin Kahl have correctly observed that retrenchment would undoubtedly heighten American reliance on that country as the strongest, most pro-U.S. partner in an endemically unstable region. "While some advocates of offshore balancing are highly critical of America's special relationship with Israel," they write, "it is worth noting that, in practice, the approach would have to rely on and work indirectly through allies such as Israel to help uphold a regional balance of power favorable to U.S. interests."[68] In these respects, offshore balancing would actually mean redoubling certain U.S. policies that have long provoked terrorist attacks.

Offshore balancing has troubling implications for counterterrorism in other respects, too. Terrorist groups like al-Qaeda prosper amid instability and security vacuums; such instability and vacuums, in turn, unwittingly can be encouraged by the premature withdrawal of U.S. military power from troubled areas. One illustration of this phenomenon would be the U.S. drawdown in Iraq in 2011, which demonstrated that the removal of American forces from a still unstable context could undercut previous counterterrorism gains and facilitate the insecurity in which jihadist organizations thrive. Although that move was generally consistent with offshore balancers' desire for reduced American military exposure in the Gulf, it ended up facilitating the renewed destabilization of large swaths of Iraq and the emergence of the Islamic State (IS) as a potent force in that area. "Had a residual U.S. force stayed in Iraq after 2011," one senior adviser to the U.S. military in Iraq has written:

> the United States would have had far greater insight into the growing threat posed by ISIS [the Islamic States in Iraq and Syria] and could have helped the Iraqis stop the group from taking so much territory. Instead, ISIS' march across northern Iraq took Washington almost completely by surprise.[69]

Withdrawal, in other words, does not always lead to a reduced terrorist threat — its effects can sometimes cut in the opposite direction.

Finally, offshore balancing would simultaneously make it more difficult to respond effectively to large-scale terrorism by corroding the infrastructure and partnerships that America has long employed to do so. As Robert Art observes, the conduct of Operation ENDURING FREEDOM in Afghanistan after 9/11 depended extensively on just those overseas bases and units that would likely be reduced or eliminated as Washington slashed its forward presence. (Since 2014, U.S. military operations against the IS have utilized many of these same assets.) In an offshore balancing scenario, by contrast, America "would have to start from scratch to build alliances and gain access to bases, a difficult and problematic process" that would likely lengthen the timeline and reduce the impact of U.S. response. In the same vein, U.S. forward deployments and security commitments have long fostered the relationships and leverage that American officials can use to obtain greater cooperation in the "quieter phase of fighting terrorism" — the diplomatic collaboration, intelligence liaison, and other largely out-of-sight measures that are crucial to defeating jihadist organizations.[70] Were America significantly to retract its security posture, one could reasonably surmise that the relationships and leverage would erode as well.

Writing in 2010, Daniel Byman observed that large-scale military retrenchment "would likely have mixed results on the threat of terrorism, some of which are difficult to predict with certainty and a few of which could prove exceptionally dangerous."[71] This appraisal still seems appropriate today. Offshore balancing offers no panaceas when it comes to counterterrorism. Its advantages are not nearly as clear-cut as one might think, and significant perils and liabilities lurk just beneath the surface. As will be seen, that pattern is even more pronounced when it comes to another security issue that offshore balancers emphasize: nuclear proliferation.

Exaggerated Security Benefits: Nuclear Proliferation.

The idea that U.S. presence and assertiveness actually motivate nuclear proliferation is a consensus view among offshore balancers, and as with the origins of terrorism, there is a certain ring of truth to the argument. As political scientists like Kenneth Waltz and Nuno Monteiro have long understood, the very fact of American military dominance creates incentives for weaker rivals to seek nuclear weapons as a means of ensuring their own security. "There is only one way

that a country can reliably deter a dominant power,"
Waltz once noted, "and that is by developing its own
nuclear force."[72]

This assertion is borne out by historical evidence,
as is the idea that the way that the United States uses
its power has sometimes added to proliferation incentives. During the 1950s, China began its pursuit of the
bomb largely in order to address the security threat
posed by U.S. presence in East Asia and to resist coercion over Taiwan and other matters. "In today's world,
if we don't want to be bullied, then we cannot do without this thing," Mao Zedong declared amid repeated
confrontations with Washington.[73] More recently, and
as the National Intelligence Council correctly predicted beforehand, the U.S. decision to invade Iraq in 2003
seems to have had the adverse results with respect to
proliferation—in particular, by driving the North Ko-
rean and Iranian governments to intensify their own
nuclear efforts so as to afford themselves some protection against suffering Saddam Hussein's fate.[74]

Yet if U.S. strategy has periodically pushed its
rivals toward the bomb, there is again much reason
to doubt that adopting offshore balancing would significantly redress the proliferation problem. To begin
with, even though American policy may be one reason why "rogue states" pursue nuclear arsenals, there
are many other reasons as well. Academic scholarship
demonstrates that there are numerous motives that
influence nuclear proliferation, ranging from desires
for international or domestic prestige, to bureaucratic
pressures, to ambitions to wield nuclear weapons as
tools of offensive or coercive leverage.[75] Saddam Hussein's quest for nuclear weapons in the late-1970s and
1980s, for example, was envisioned not just as an effort to achieve defensive deterrence against rivals like

Israel, but also as a means of underwriting aggressive, revisionist initiatives vis-à-vis that country. Nuclear weapons, Saddam once commented, would allow Iraq to "guarantee the long war that is destructive to our enemy, and take at our leisure each meter of land and drown the enemy with rivers of blood."[76] Similarly complex motives have figured in other cases of nuclear proliferation. The drivers of that phenomenon, like the drivers of terrorism, are more multi-faceted than offshore balancers believe, and so altering American strategy would address but one aspect of the challenge.

More likely, offshore balancing would make matters worse, because it would forfeit the leverage and influence that Washington traditionally has employed to restrain widespread proliferation. Whatever their pitfalls, U.S. forward presence and security commitments have, on the whole, exerted a powerful restraining effect on the spread of nuclear weapons. As both academics and government officials have recognized, U.S. security guarantees and troop deployments provide reassurance that drastically reduces the need for American allies to seek safety in independent nuclear arsenals. Those arrangements, the Obama administration's 2010 *Nuclear Posture Review* noted, limit proliferation "by reassuring non-nuclear U.S. allies and partners that their security interests can be protected without their own nuclear deterrent capabilities."[77] Conversely, the implicit—and sometimes explicit—threat that U.S. guarantees and presence might be rescinded if an ally chooses to go nuclear offers a "stick" that can be, and has been, used to dissuade aspiring proliferators.[78] Finally, and no less important, the United States can use its position of centrality in the international system—a position that rests largely on its role as provider of security in key regions—to spearhead other nonproliferation initiatives, such as efforts to constrict the supply of critical nuclear components and materials, and to sanction aspiring proliferators.[79]

To be clear, these are not merely abstract or theoretical advantages of America's long-standing approach to grand strategy. Rather, a host of academic research demonstrates that in case after case during the postwar decades, this combination of elements has been vital to keeping proliferation as relatively limited as it has been. During the Cold War, this mixture of carrots and sticks played a vital role in preventing countries from West Germany and Sweden, to Australia, South Korea, Taiwan, and Japan, from taking the decisive steps needed to obtain nuclear weapons.[80] After the Cold War, realist scholars like John Mearsheimer predicted that the collapse of bipolarity would lead to widespread proliferation in key regions like Europe.[81] The continued provision of reassurance by the United States helped contain this threat, however, and as Mark Kramer has written, the promise of robust security guarantees from NATO helped dampen the proliferation pressures that might otherwise have arisen in Poland and other former Warsaw Pact states.[82] American security commitments and alliances, one recent survey aptly concludes, "have been arguably the most important and consequential of the strategies of [nonproliferation]."[83]

What effect would a shift to offshore balancing have on proliferation dynamics? As offshore balancers argue, retracting U.S. presence and posture might ease some pressures for nuclear proliferation among American rivals. The number of those countries is quite small, however, and it is hard to see how, in practice, retrenchment would reverse the well-advanced nuclear programs of countries like North Korea. What significant U.S. retrenchment **could** quite plausibly do is to dramatically exacerbate the pressures for proliferation in a broader and more meaningful sense. In East Asia, a U.S. pullback would accentuate insecurity on the part of countries that are contending with a more assertive China, and whose nuclear forbearance has long been inextricably linked to the American presence.[84] In the Middle East, Iran's nuclear progress has already stirred proliferation impulses in countries like Saudi Arabia and the United Arab Emirates; those impulses would likely become far more difficult to repress were U.S. reassurance weakened.[85] Even in a region like Eastern Europe, one can easily imagine how the destabilizing mix of U.S. retrenchment and Russian aggressiveness could lead a technologically adept, and deeply security-conscious, country like Poland to consider pursuing its own nuclear option. Throughout the key geopolitical regions, offshore balancing would run considerable risk of heightening proliferation incentives and encouraging a more nuclearized world.[86]

That world, in turn, would probably be more dangerous and unstable than the one we currently inhabit. Some offshore balancers, hailing from the tradition of defensive realism, argue that the emergence of more nuclear-armed states will lead to the establishment of effective deterrence between adversaries and result in greater geopolitical stability.[87] Yet a growing body of academic research, as well as basic common sense, cast doubt on this sanguine outlook. More nuclear capabilities might mean more chances for nuclear terrorism or nuclear accidents.[88] Proliferating states might not develop the secure second-strike and command-and-control capabilities that are essential to decreasing first-strike incentives and ensuring stable deterrence.[89] Recent scholarly work also suggests that proliferation can increase the propensity for conflict in affected regions, and that it causes the rulers of proliferating states to behave more aggressively in the period following acquisition of nuclear weapons.[90] Especially if a U.S. withdrawal leads to intensified security competitions in key regions—and as discussed later, there is good reason to think that it might—the results could be perilous indeed.

In sum, when offshore balancing is subjected to greater scrutiny, it no longer looks like such a bargain where proliferation is concerned. For rather than alleviating a major challenge to U.S. interests and international stability, it might very well increase that challenge instead.

Impact on U.S. Influence and Global Stability.

Offshore balancing, then, would probably not pay great dividends on essential security issues like terrorism and nuclear proliferation, and, in key respects, it would likely cause more harm than good. But how does offshore balancing fare when one considers the broader and even more crucial issue at hand—the question of how successful that strategy will be in preserving U.S. global influence and maintaining a comparatively stable and advantageous international environment? A core assumption of offshore balancing is that retrenchment will not imperil that environment. Offshore balancers believe that a more circumspect grand strategy will lessen great power frictions, compel free-riding American allies to bear more of the load, and thus sustain basic global stability at a reduced price. As noted earlier, some proponents of the strategy also believe that offshore balancing will, counterintuitively, enhance American influence overseas. Here as elsewhere, the central claim of offshore balancing is that less activism and engagement will produce equal or even better results. Here as elsewhere, however, that argument is deeply suspect.

Grasping this point requires understanding that offshore balancers' critique of the inherited U.S. strategy is considerably overdrawn. From reading arguments in favor of offshore balancing, one often gets the impression that American strategy actively undercuts the nation's influence and interests, by eliciting widespread systemic resistance and making Washington more enemies than friends. Yet the reality is not nearly so bleak. Yes, American power and interventions undoubtedly appear threatening to U.S. rivals, and certain post-Cold War endeavors—particularly the invasion of Iraq—were highly unpopular overseas.[91] But even so, it is misleading to suggest that American policy causes such widespread, systematic alienation and pushback as offshore balancers believe.

As several leading scholars have noted, for example, the importance of anti-U.S. "soft balancing" is frequently exaggerated, because empirical support for that phenomenon is actually quite weak, and because it is really Washington that most frequently utilizes the tools of "soft balancing"—international institutions, diplomatic coalition-building, and others—to achieve its foreign-policy preferences.[92] Moreover, and contrary to what one might expect from reading the offshore balancing literature, the dominant tendency of the post-Cold War era has been for countries to align with, rather than against, America. This has been true in Europe, where the United States has not simply maintained NATO but taken on 12 additional allies since the outset of the unipolar period. It has also been true in Asia, where American defense, security, and political relationships have frequently been upgraded, intensified, and expanded since the mid-1990s. Even during the George W. Bush administration — the years when anti-American sentiment was probably at its peak — Washington actually increased and improved its security ties with a wide range of second- and third-tier states that saw American influence not as a threat but as a source of reassurance and protection vis-à-vis rising regional powers like Russia and China. Certain American policies may elicit widespread global disapproval, but the recent trend has been one of "balancing with" the United States rather than "balancing against it."[93]

Far from being a geopolitical liability, in fact, America's forward presence and engagement have long been deeply interlinked with both U.S. influence and international stability. On the subject of influence, the security that America has provided its friends and allies has, in turn, provided America with substantial leverage in shaping those partners' policies. "The more U.S. troops are stationed in a country," one statistical analysis of this question finds, "the more closely that country's foreign policy orientation aligns with that of the United States."[94] Historical evidence supports this assertion. From the early Cold War to the present, U.S. officials have often invoked the sway afforded by America's forward presence to prevent allies from pursuing nuclear weapons, to gain more beneficial terms in trade and financial pacts, and even to impact the makeup of its allies' governments.[95] In the trade and financial realm, for instance, U.S. troop presence provided a bargaining chip that Washington employed to get NATO allies to bolster the dollar during the 1960s. Over 40 years later, the U.S.-South Korea security relationship provided leverage that American negotiators used to obtain better terms in the U.S.-South Korea Free Trade Agreement.[96] More broadly, American alliances have served as mechanisms for influencing economic, political, and security agendas in key regions, and for projecting Washington's voice on a wide array of matters. Admittedly, that voice might not be as strong as U.S. officials desire or some international observers believe, but it has nonetheless been quite powerful and pervasive by any meaningful comparison.

The relative international stability of the postwar period has an equally intimate relationship with America's global posture. As even some advocates of retrenchment concede, the fact that historically war-prone regions like Europe have remained comparatively peaceful in recent decades is not primarily a function of any dramatic advance in human enlightenment. Rather, that phenomenon has owed largely to the way that the "American pacifier" has soothed just those destabilizing impulses that previously caused upheaval and war. In key strategic regions, the U.S. presence has suppressed arms races and geopolitical competitions by affording the security that permits other countries effectively to underbuild their armed forces. Likewise, it has eased long-standing historical antagonisms by providing the atmosphere of reassurance in which powerful nations like Japan and Germany could be reinvigorated economically and reintegrated into functioning regional orders. Finally, the U.S. presence has been a force for moderation in the conduct of both allies and adversaries, deterring outright aggression and discouraging other forms of disruptive behavior. America "effectively acts as a night watchman," Mearsheimer acknowledges, a geopolitical "Leviathan" that brings order and stability to an otherwise anarchical realm.[97] "The contribution that the United States makes" to preventing the febrile international instability of earlier eras, another prominent political scientist observes, "is similar to the services that governments provide within sovereign states."[98]

What consequences would follow if the United States retracted the presence and commitments that have permitted it to play this role? While the future cannot be predicted with certainty, the most logical and obvious result would be to imperil influence and stability alike. On the former issue, it is simply not clear why American influence in other countries' and regions' affairs would persist—much less expand—if the policies and presence that have so long enabled that influence were abandoned. It seems far more probable that actors who no longer benefitted from such strong and visible U.S. support would have considerably less reason to defer to American wishes, just as it seems probable that the weakening or termination of U.S. alliances would leave Washington with diminished ability to exert leadership in crucial regions. Likewise, a major geopolitical pullback could make it more difficult to maintain the regular international military training and exercises that expand American reach by promoting interoperability with friends and partners.[99] In effect, forward presence and security commitments have been the currency that Washington uses to buy a good portion of its international influence. A broad-based retrenchment would presumably devalue that currency and weaken other mechanisms that Washington has traditionally used to shape relationships and project its global voice.

Retrenchment would seem a little less dangerous when it comes to international stability. Offshore
balancers may be right to predict that their strategy
would compel local or regional powers to devote additional resources to defense, and perhaps mitigate
certain issues of contention with those nations that
are currently antagonized by U.S. presence.[100] Cutting
Taiwan loose would certainly remove one potential
flashpoint vis-à-vis China; reducing or eliminating
the American military presence in Europe might indeed meet with Russian approbation. The problem,
alas, is that it is also logical to expect that removing
the American pacifier would unleash the more pernicious impulses that U.S. presence traditionally has
suppressed. Security competitions that have long lain
dormant might reawaken and intensify as countries
more actively built up their own military capabilities.
Long-repressed national rivalries might reignite following the elimination of strong American presence
and the reassurance it offers. Additionally, while revisionist powers that dislike existing orders in Europe,
the Persian Gulf, or East Asia would probably take a
positive view of American retrenchment, they might
just as likely exploit the retraction of U.S. power to assert their own claims more forcefully. In sum, if one
accepts Mearsheimer's own view that Washington
has long played Leviathan in crucial regions, then it
is hard to dispute the corresponding concern: "Take
away that Leviathan, and there is likely to be big
trouble."[101]

As with the question of nuclear proliferation, this is
more than a theoretical concern. It does not take much
imagination to see where and how such trouble might
reemerge today. In Europe, normally the most peaceful and stable of the three major regions, a progres-

sively more aggressive Russia is already destabilizing neighboring states, using force to redraw national boundaries, and generally contesting the post-Cold War notion of a continent whole, free, and at peace.[102] In the Middle East and particularly the Persian Gulf, growing Iranian assertiveness has provoked profound regional anxieties that have played out in proxy wars in Syria and Yemen, as well as hints of a potential arms race—all as the Gulf countries simultaneously face the instability and violence associated with the rise of the IS. Not least of all, China's ascendancy is jostling the regional order in East Asia. Beijing's territorial claims and military buildup have sparked rising tensions with its neighbors, many of which—such as South Korea and Japan—still harbor lingering historical animosities vis-à-vis one another. In the early post-Cold War period, one analyst famously argued that East Asia was "ripe for rivalry"; even with a continuing U.S. presence, that description seems increasingly apt today. Across these regional contexts, there is thus much reason to worry that the result of retrenchment would not be low-cost, post-American stability, but rather intensified turmoil and upheaval.[103]

Some offshore balancers acknowledge as much, and argue that Washington could accept—perhaps benefit from—such instability so long as it did not permit a hostile power to dominate a core region of Eurasia.[104] The trouble with this assertion is that it ignores the damage that increased global instability could inflict on important U.S. interests even if a regional hegemon did not emerge. For one thing, it seems unlikely that greater global conflict and turmoil would facilitate the intensive multilateral collaboration needed to address transnational problems ranging from climate change to pandemics to piracy. It seems just as improbable that such an atmosphere would conduce to the continued flourishing and spread of liberal democracy. Scholars widely recognize that, in places from Germany and Japan during the Cold War to Eastern Europe in the 1990s, American presence and/or guarantees helped incentivize democratic reforms and foster the security in which liberal institutions could succeed.[105] There is equally recognition that "a stable and prosperous world is more conducive to democratic spread and human rights protection than an unstable, less prosperous world."[106] Offshore balancing, therefore, would not simply downgrade the democracy-promotion initiatives that have facilitated liberalism's remarkable advance in recent decades.[107] The greater instability that would likely follow an American retrenchment could also prove quite damaging to hopes for the continued strength and spread of the political institutions that the United States prefers.

The consequences for the increasingly integrated global economy that Washington has long promoted could be just as problematic. As Michael Mandelbaum and other scholars have correctly noted, the tremendous gains toward international openness and prosperity during the postwar decades have been critically enabled by American forward presence and the relative stability and security it affords.[108] That forward presence has protected critical sea lanes and secured the global commons, while also containing the geopolitical conflicts that might, by erupting, badly disrupt an interlinked world economy. In Europe, for instance, American protection has long provided the shield behind which continental integration could occur; in East Asia, the persistence of U.S. presence after the Cold War has had the intention — and effect — of underwriting similar advances.[109] To be clear, the question of how global trade and finance would react in an atmosphere of greater instability can only be conclusively answered when such a scenario comes to pass. Yet it would seem Pollyannaish to predict that global interchange would not be affected negatively by intensifying geopolitical competition in areas of tremendous significance to an interwoven world economy.

What all of this suggests is that offshore balancing could reasonably be expected to undermine, rather than preserve, U.S. influence and international stability, and that even if America's physical safety were not directly jeopardized by post-retrenchment turmoil, some of its key national interests might be. Then there is the greatest danger that a strategy of offshore balancing would court—the danger that a crucial region might not actually be able to keep its balance absent U.S. forward presence.

Could the Balance Break?

Whether it was ultimately reversible or not, the collapse or severe deterioration of a key regional balance would have grave implications for the United States. In the worst case, such a development could produce a seismic shift in the global balance of power and negate a core goal of postwar American grand strategy. Even in the best case, it would require what would likely be a major military intervention to restore the broken balance and defeat the offending aggressor. Either way, the costs and dangers involved could easily be immense. If adopting offshore balancing could reasonably lead to heightened risks of such a scenario, there would be another strong reason to doubt that strategy's basic viability.

Offshore balancers generally believe that there is little danger of such a scenario materializing, because bids for regional hegemony will provoke a timely counterbalancing response from states within the region, and because America can move quickly to head off growing threats before they become truly critical. Viewed through the lens of history, however, these assumptions appear somewhat questionable. As mentioned previously, the fact is that "underbalancing" happens: in the world wars and the Persian Gulf War, local actors ultimately proved unable to contain aspiring regional hegemons.[110] In two of those cases — World War II and the Gulf War — the balance broke, or severely eroded, in surprisingly rapid fashion. In April 1940, it was certainly not obvious to most observers that Great Britain and France were entirely incapable of checking German power on continental Europe, and that this regional balance would have collapsed entirely within 6 weeks.[111] In mid-1990, U.S. officials only belatedly recognized that Saddam Hussein intended to conquer Kuwait and fundamentally alter the balance in the Gulf, and by the time they came to that realization, there was essentially nothing they could do to impede the Iraqi assault. (Nor, in the days following the invasion, was there much that U.S. forces could have done to impede a follow-on attack into Saudi Arabia.)[112] The belief that regional balances are inherently robust and that Washington can see adverse shifts coming in time to prevent them without having to fight a major war is thus shakier than it seems.

Since the early-1990s, of course, the global security environment has been comparatively benign by historical standards, and so the prospect that a hostile regional hegemon might again emerge has seemed far

48

more remote. Even today, there is very little near-term likelihood that any U.S. adversary could marshal the power to dominate Europe, East Asia, or the Persian Gulf, even if America left those regions entirely to their own devices. Looking toward the medium- and long-range future, however, there is at least one rising power that might seriously threaten the existing balance within its region.

That country, obviously, is China. Today, China still falls well short of the level of power needed to assert regional dominance even in the absence of U.S. presence.[113] Moreover, it is not clear that China will aspire to such regional dominance as its power increases. Yet a peaceful rise cannot be guaranteed, either, and China's ability to pursue regional primacy could increase markedly in the decades to come. Explosive economic growth and a long-term military buildup have already had a pronounced impact on the military balance vis-à-vis neighbors like Taiwan, Vietnam, the Philippines, and Japan. If Chinese economic growth continues apace, and if China's defense budget continues to register annual increases of 10 percent or more, then other East Asian countries will eventually confront enormous difficulty in balancing Beijing's power — even if they overcome collective action problems and their own historical antagonisms to cooperate in that undertaking. This prospect is one that is clearly recognized even by some leading proponents of American retrenchment. As one offshore balancer puts it, "The United States will have to play a key role in countering China, because its Asian neighbors are not strong enough to do it by themselves."[114]

Yet if this assessment is accurate — and there is every reason to think that it is — then offshore balancing becomes a highly risky and potentially counterproductive course of action. As noted, some analysts have argued that adopting that strategy would actually improve Washington's ability to counter Chinese power, by strengthening U.S. flexibility, better leveraging the capabilities of local actors, and divesting America of distracting onshore commitments in other regions. But here again, this analysis glosses over a range of more worrisome possibilities. As mentioned earlier, U.S. retrenchment could motivate exposed local actors like South Korea or Japan to pursue their own nuclear arsenals, thereby impelling regional arms races and heightening tensions further. Or, perhaps more dangerously still, a U.S. pullback might facilitate the very outcome that offshore balancers aim to avert. As Robert Gilpin wrote in his classic work, *War and Change in World Politics*:

> Retrenchment by its very nature is an indication of relative weakness and declining power, and thus retrenchment can have a deteriorating effect on relations with allies and rivals. Sensing the decline of their protector, allies try to obtain the best deal they can from the rising master of the system. Rivals are stimulated to 'close in,' and frequently they precipitate a conflict in the process.

Retrenchment can be carried out successfully, Gilpin acknowledges, but in a charged geopolitical environment it is usually a fraught and perilous path.[115]

This warning has particular salience in the East Asian context. In that region, U.S. allies as well as formally nonaligned countries count on American support and presence to help them manage their relationships with an increasingly powerful, and increasingly abrasive, Beijing. As analysts like Zachary Selden have observed, these countries seek visible U.S. backing and reassurance precisely because they fear that they could not otherwise balance a rising China. "America is now an alternative to China," said one Vietnamese observer as early as 2000. "To counter the Chinese threat we must lean toward the West."[116] Similar comments have become ubiquitous in the years since then.

In these circumstances, and contrary to what offshore balancers expect, a significant American retrenchment might not have the desired effect of compelling these countries to resist more determinedly and successfully potential Chinese expansion. Instead, it might incentivize them to acquiesce to, or perhaps bandwagon with, an assertive Beijing if they calculated that the odds of effective resistance were declining as Washington pulled back. If U.S. presence in Asia were weakened, one Thai commentator has predicted, Asian countries would have to conclude that "the region will no longer be a place where only one major power plays a dominant role," and hedge their bets accordingly. Likewise, one analysis of U.S. security relationships concludes that while reducing the American military presence in the Pacific might bring some budgetary savings, "in Vietnam, Australia, or the Philippines . . . such a shift could prompt a wholesale reevaluation of national defense policy and have costly implications."[117] In sum, if one expects that Asian countries will have great difficulty checking Chinese power without U.S. assistance, then reducing Washington's role in the area could actually discourage local balancing and pave the way for Beijing's ascent.[118]

Offshore balancing could plausibly encourage this undesirable outcome in other ways, as well. As Gilpin notes, when retrenchment is viewed as weakness or lack of commitment, it can cause revisionist powers to push harder against the contours of the existing order. This danger cannot be ignored in the Asia-Pacific. There is evidence to suggest, as offshore balancers argue, that a desire to counteract U.S. presence and security commitments in the region has been an important motivator of China's post-Cold War military buildup.[119] Yet there is also evidence to suggest that U.S. presence and commitments nonetheless have had an overall tempering effect on Chinese behavior, by limiting opportunities for intimidation and expansion, and by raising the likely costs of aggressive or destabilizing behavior.[120] If the United States were to now begin reducing that presence, it might logically undercut the tempering effect in the process, for a U.S. retrenchment would have the practical consequence of accentuating the growing power disparity between Beijing and its neighbors, and creating greater uncertainty in Chinese minds as to whether Washington would actually come to those countries' defense in a crisis. The upshot could be to incentivize precisely the sort of expansionist behavior that would challenge the regional order.[121]

Finally, if an offshore balancing type approach might therefore encourage adverse shifts in the regional equilibrium, it would equally complicate U.S. efforts to respond to those shifts. Offshore balancing assumes that the United States would be able to intervene adeptly to prevent such changes (or to reverse them if they did occur), and that retrenching from other regions would provide greater flexibility and leverage in addressing adverse events in the Asia-Pacific. But the crucial flaw in the logic of retrenchment is that going offshore generally makes it harder rather than easier to affect the regional equilibrium.[122] Right now, U.S. forward presence affords America a number of critical advantages that it can draw on in shaping the regional climate in East Asia and responding to crises should they emerge: strong and deeply institutionalized alliances; established patterns of basing, logistics, and access; high degrees of interoperability that come through near-continual training with friendly militaries; and others. These assets not only help check Chinese power and hedge against unwelcome developments in peacetime. They would also serve as the indispensable foundation of Washington's response should the region nonetheless descend into conflict, providing a preexisting framework and infrastructure for large-scale U.S. intervention.

Were these assets to be devalued or liquidated via retrenchment, however, then the United States would face a far greater challenge. In peacetime, it would possess fewer of the instruments and arrangements that have long allowed it to influence the behavior of allies and adversaries, and head off unfavorable events before they occur. In wartime, the disadvantages would be greater still. The United States would face the daunting prospect of assembling the necessary coalitions, access, and basing agreements on the fly. It would confront the problems inherent in working with foreign governments and militaries with which it had less familiarity and fewer ongoing ties. It would have to overcome the considerable logistical challenges of moving a greater proportion of the required forces into theater, and perhaps fighting its way back into a region after an adversary had exploited U.S. absence to stake out a more formidable position there. And, of course, it would have to do all of this amid the intense pressure of a brewing or ongoing conflict. "Getting out of the marginal seas might be easy," two experts on naval strategy conclude. "Getting back in would be a different proposition entirely."[123] Or, as another leading scholar appropriately puts it, "Beefing up a preexisting presence in an emergency is easier than re-establishing one from scratch in a crisis."[124]

Offshore balancers would do well to keep these warnings in mind. The strategy they recommend promises to preserve regional balances at reduced costs. But instead, it might well heighten the risk of dangerous developments in a key region like East Asia, while simultaneously exacerbating the hazards and difficulties of an American response.[125]

CONCLUSION

Is offshore balancing truly an idea whose time has come? Does that grand strategy represent the right path forward for America? A growing number of observers in the strategic studies and policy communities believe that this is the case. They argue that America's long-standing postwar grand strategy has outlived its utility, and that the danger to U.S. interests now lies not in doing too little, but rather in doing too much. Accordingly, they believe that adopting the more restrained global posture entailed by offshore balancing can actually produce superior overall outcomes at a bargain price. This "less can be more" ethos has proven quite attractive in the post-Iraq, post-financial crisis context, and it has given offshore balancing an increasing currency and prominence in debates on the future of Washington's stance toward the world. As two informed analysts have written, "Who could object to a strategy designed to reduce costs and risks to the United States, bolster America's good name in foreign capitals, and encourage Eurasian states to manage their own affairs?"[126]

All that glitters is not gold, however, and, upon closer inspection, the luster of offshore balancing fades considerably. Proponents of that strategy have certainly performed a valuable service in illuminating certain downsides of America's current global posture, and in forcing defenders of that posture to clarify and more persuasively articulate their arguments.[127] Yet as this monograph has demonstrated, the case for shifting to offshore balancing is ultimately much weaker than it might first appear. Across a broad range of crucial issues—from budgetary impact, to key security threats like terrorism and nuclear proliferation, to the retention of American global influence and a stable and congenial international environment—the probable advantages of large-scale retrenchment are less significant than frequently advertised. The probable disadvantages, by contrast, are quite significant and compelling. Offshore balancing may purport to be a near-optimal grand strategy that can deliver low-cost security, stability, and influence for the United States. Yet, were Washington actually to adopt that approach, the more plausible the outcome might well be to endanger precisely the security, stability, and influence that American statecraft traditionally has provided, and to swap relatively modest near-term economies for a host of sobering long-term risks and costs.

The analysis presented here thus argues strongly against a turn to offshore balancing as America's grand strategy. More broadly, it argues for a healthy dose of skepticism in evaluating proposals for a major departure from the core patterns of postwar U.S. statecraft. As the current popularity of offshore balancing illustrates, at times of geopolitical difficulty and constraint, it can be tempting to seek refuge in a sort of grand strategic panacea: in this case, an approach that promises to maintain the essential blessings of the post-1945 order without imposing the long-standing costs and requirements of sustaining that order. Yet the unfortunate reality is that panaceas rarely pan out, and in the case of offshore balancing, it quickly becomes apparent that one cannot easily shed the burdens of U.S. postwar strategy without endangering the benefits as well. As the debate over America's current and future global role continues, it will therefore be advisable to maintain a high standard of proof in evaluating proposals for a significant shift in American strategy. For while less can indeed sometimes be more, in grand strategy as in many things, less is usually just less.[128]

What does all of this mean with respect to the U.S. Army in particular, and with respect to American Landpower in general? At a minimum, it means that the United States will continue to possess a compelling strategic rationale for maintaining robust, readily deployable ground forces capable of projecting power and presence in crucial regions around the world. To be clear, the maintenance of American forward presence, and the projection of American power, has been and will remain a task for all of the services, and one that involves air, sea, and ground forces alike. Moreover, just as the role of American Landpower expanded at the margins during the manpower intensive conflicts in Iraq and Afghanistan following 2001, it has been natural and appropriate to undertake some rebalancing of the joint force more recently, as such conflicts have come to play a less dominant role in U.S. military and defense strategy. Yet just as the United States would be unwise to embrace a dramatic retrenchment in its overall geopolitical posture, it would be no less unwise to heed calls for drastic cuts—up to 50 percent, as proposed by some analysts—in its ground forces.[129]

The reasons for this are manifold, but the basic underlying theme is that U.S. Landpower remains essential to delivering the benefits that the legacy grand strategy has long provided, and that offshore balancing would likely jeopardize. Through their forward presence, U.S. ground forces often represent the embodiment of both reassurance and deterrence, by providing a very tangible manifestation of Washington's commitment to a given country or region. They enable regular training and exercises with partner nations, thereby improving U.S. relationships and influence in peacetime, and promoting crucial interoperability in times of crisis. Not least of all, they constitute a strategic hedge against unfavorable geopolitical developments, and a means of meeting those developments early, should they nonetheless materialize. One recent white paper on strategic Landpower puts it aptly:

> Forward deployed, actively engaged forces have proven essential to contributing to peace by reassuring our friends and deterring our enemies. Such forces provide a broad range of benefits that includes: demonstration of U.S. commitment, establishment of enduring relationships with regional military and political leaders, improved capabilities of hosts to handle their own internal security challenges, increased willingness of hosts to participate in friendly coalitions, ability of the U.S. to achieve a higher level of understanding than is possible just with technical means, reduced chance of experiencing strategic surprise, reduced change that an aggressor will miscalculate U.S. resolve or capability, and increased responsiveness to crises.

If the United States seeks to avoid the geopolitical dangers associated with large-scale retrenchment, it will need to retain strong, effective Landpower as a key part of a balanced joint force.[130]

To conclude by returning to the broader grand strategic picture, it merits stating explicitly that this analysis is not meant to foreclose the possibility of any adaptation, flexibility, or retrenchment in Washington's approach to international affairs. As the events of the post-9/11 years made quite apparent, when it comes to grand strategy, too much assertiveness can be just as dangerous as too much restraint. And as recent scholarship has underscored, any successful grand strategy — whether within a given presidential administration, or over a longer period of time — virtually always entails some degree of change within continuity.[131] Indeed, the postwar grand strategy has itself featured a process of near-continual refinement at the margins, as American policymakers have adapted to shifting challenges and circumstances, and corrected for prior underreach or overreach, while still affirming the basic underlying approach of energetic global engagement.[132] This was the tack taken by the Dwight Eisenhower administration upon inheriting President Harry Truman's costly conflict in Korea, for example, and by the Richard Nixon administration as it sought to grapple with American overextension in Vietnam.[133] One needs to look no further than the Obama administration's recent policies to see this dynamic at work today. Since taking power in 2009, that administration consistently has affirmed the imperative of U.S. global engagement and leadership, even as it has also sought to rebalance that engagement geographically, and to avoid the large-scale, protracted military interventions that characterized its predecessor's approach.[134]

This process of strategic adjustment — as opposed to a wholesale change of strategy — will continue to be necessary in the coming years, so as to preserve the myriad advantages of America's postwar posture, while still allowing U.S. statecraft to adapt to the changes that invariably occur in the international environment. Precisely what such adjustment might look like in practice is beyond the scope of this monograph, as this subject would require an extended treatment of its own. Yet it is worth noting that informed analysts such as Peter Feaver, Bruce Jentleson, and Robert Art have already mooted various proposals for how the United States might effectively refine and recalibrate its traditional approach, so as to better reflect current constraints, problems, and opportunities.[135] Looking to the future, American officials would do well to focus their energies on accomplishing this familiar task of accommodating inevitable change within a framework of broader continuity. As this monograph has argued, they would do equally well to reject the more extreme option of broad-based retrenchment, and to resist the tempting but false allure of offshore balancing.

ENDNOTES

1. A shorter version of the argument presented here appears as Hal Brands, "Fools Rush Out? The Flawed Logic of Offshore Balancing," *The Washington Quarterly*, Vol. 38, No. 2, Summer 2015. The ideas presented in this monograph have been considerably developed and expanded from that shorter publication.

2. The literature in support of offshore balancing is immense, reflecting the support that concept commands within the academy. A nonexhaustive list of key texts would include Stephen Walt, "The End of the American Era," *National Interest*, No. 116, November/December 2011, pp. 6-16; Walt, "In the National Interest: A New Grand Strategy for American Foreign Policy," *Boston Review*, February/March 2005, available from *bostonreview.net/BR30.1/walt.php*, accessed February 12, 2015; Walt, *Taming American Power: The Global Response to U.S. Primacy*, New York: Norton, 2006; Robert Pape, *Dying to Win: The Strategic Logic of Suicide*

Terrorism, New York, NY: Random House, 2005, esp. pp. 237-250; Pape, "Empire Falls," *National Interest*, No. 99, January/February 2009, pp. 21-34; Barry Posen, "The Case for Restraint," *American Interest*, Vol. 3, No. 2, November/December 2007, pp. 7-17; Posen, "Pull Back: The Case for a Less Activist Foreign Policy," *Foreign Affairs*, Vol. 92, No. 1, January/February 2013, pp. 116-129; Posen, *Restraint: A New Foundation for U.S. Grand Strategy*, Ithaca, NY: Cornell University Press, 2014; Eugene Gholz and Daryl Press, "Footprints in the Sand," *American Interest*, Vol. 5., No. 4, March/April 2010, pp. 59-67; Christopher Layne, *The Peace of Illusions: American Grand Strategy from 1940 to the Present*, Ithaca, NY: Cornell University Press, 2006, pp. 159-192; Layne, "From Preponderance to Offshore Balancing: America's Future Grand Strategy," *International Security*, Vol. 22, No. 1, Summer 1997, pp. 86-124; Layne, "Offshore Balancing Revisited, *Washington Quarterly*, Vol. 25, No. 2, Spring 2002, pp. 233-248; Benjamin Schwartz and Christopher Layne, "A New Grand Strategy," *Atlantic Monthly*, January 2002, pp. 36-42; Eugene Gholz, Daryl Press, and Harvey Sapolsky, "Come Home, America: The Strategy of Restraint in the Face of Temptation," *International Security*, Vol. 21, No. 4, Spring 1997, pp. 5-48; John Mearsheimer, "Imperial by Design," *National Interest*, No. 111, January/February 2011, pp. 16-34. See also the works cited hereafter. It is worth noting that some of these scholars do not explicitly use the term "offshore balancing" to describe their preferred strategy, and they occasionally disagree on specific policy prescriptions. Generally speaking, however, the underlying strategy they recommend is the same.

3. Christopher Layne, "The (Almost) Triumph of Offshore Balancing," *National Interest*, January 27, 2012, available from *nationalinterest.org/commentary/almost-triumph-offshore-balancing-6405*, accessed February 24, 2015.

4. Stephen Walt, "Offshore Balancing: An Idea Whose Time Has Come," *Foreign Policy*, November 2, 2011, available from *foreignpolicy.com/2011/11/02/offshore-balancing-an-idea-whose-time-has-come/*, accessed February 24, 2015. See also Peter Beinart, "Obama's Foreign Policy Doctrine Finally Emerges with 'Offshore Balancing'," *The Daily Beast*, November 28, 2011, available from *www.thedailybeast.com/articles/2011/11/28/obama-s-foreign-policy-doctrine-finally-emerges-with-off-shore-balancing.html*, accessed February 25, 2015; Walt, "A Bandwagon for Offshore Balanc-

ing?" *Foreign Policy*, December 1, 2011, available from *foreign-policy.com/2011/12/01/a-bandwagon-for-offshore-balancing/*, accessed February 25, 2015.

5. For one insightful exception from more than a decade ago, see Robert Art, *A Grand Strategy for America*, Ithaca, NY: Cornell University Press, 2002, esp. pp. 176-177, 181-222. For a more recent but theater-specific critique, see James Holmes and Toshi Yoshihara, "An Ocean Too Far: Offshore Balancing in the Indian Ocean," *Asian Security*, Vol. 8, No. 1, March 2012, pp. 1-26. For a historical perspective on the strategy, see Williamson Murray and Peter Mansoor, "U.S. Grand Strategy in the 21st Century: The Case for a Continental Commitment," *Orbis*, Vol. 59, No. 1, Winter 2015, pp. 19-34.

6. For a good discussion of grand strategic choices and options facing the United States, see Richard Fontaine and Kristin Lord, eds., *America's Path: Grand Strategy for the Next Administration*, Washington, DC: Center for a New American Security, 2012.

7. Walt, "In the National Interest."

8. Latin America, of course, has also long been considered a crucial region for U.S. security interests, and the United States has rarely hesitated to act assertively in that region when those interests are perceived to be at risk. But since Washington's dominance in that region traditionally has been so pronounced, the United States has generally not felt the need to retain such large-scale, permanent military presence in the region, at least not during the post-World War II era.

9. The best discussion and defense of postwar strategy is Stephen G. Brooks, G. John Ikenberry, and William Wohlforth, "Don't Come Home, America: The Case against Retrenchment," *International Security*, Vol. 37, No. 3, Winter 2012/13, pp. 7-51, quoted on p. 11. See also Robert Kagan, *The World America Made*, New York: Vintage, 2012, pp. 16-68; John Lewis Gaddis, *Strategies of Containment: A Critical Appraisal of American National Security Policy during the Cold War*, New York: Oxford University Press, 2005.

10. The origins of and reasons for America's postwar strategy are discussed in Melvyn Leffler, *A Preponderance of Power: National Security, The Truman Administration, and the Cold War*, Stanford, CA: Stanford University Press, 1992; G. John Ikenberry, *After Victory: Institutions, Strategic Restraint, and the Rebuilding of Order after Major Wars*, Princeton, NJ: Princeton University Press, 2001, pp. 163-214. On the nuclear issue in particular, see Francis Gavin, "Strategies of Inhibition: American Grand Strategy and the Nuclear Revolution," *International Security*, forthcoming, 2015.

11. See Melvyn Leffler, "Dreams of Freedom, Temptations of Power," in Jeffrey Engel, ed., *The Fall of the Berlin Wall: The Revolutionary Legacy of 1989*, New York: Oxford University Press, 2009, esp. pp. 146-147.

12. A good description of post-Cold War strategy is Peter Feaver and Stephen Biddle, "Assessing Strategic Choices in the War on Terror," in James Burk, ed., *How 9/11 Changed Our Ways of War*, Stanford, CA: Stanford University Press, 2014, pp. 29-31. On the shaping of that strategy, see also Hal Brands, *Making the Unipolar Moment: U.S. Foreign Policy and the Rise of the Post-Cold War Order*, Ithaca, NY: Cornell University Press, forthcoming 2016; Brands, *From Berlin to Baghdad: America's Search for Purpose in the Post-Cold War World*, Lexington, KY: University Press of Kentucky, 2008, esp. chapters 2-3.

13. See G. John Ikenberry, *Liberal Leviathan: The Origins, Crisis, and Transformation of the American World Order*, Princeton, NJ: Princeton University Press, 2012, esp. pp. 159-220; Tony Smith, *America's Mission: The United States and the Worldwide Struggle for Democracy in the Twentieth Century*, Princeton, NJ: Princeton University Press, 1994.

14. See Gaddis, *Strategies of Containment*; also Michael Mandelbaum, *The Case for Goliath: How America Acts as the World's Government in the 21st Century*, New York: Public Affairs, 2006, esp. pp. 31-87.

15. Gavin, "Strategies of Inhibition"; also Nicholas Miller, "Hegemony and Nuclear Proliferation," Ph.D. Dissertation, Massachusetts Institute of Technology, Cambridge, MA, 2014.

16. Gholz, Press, and Sapolsky, "Come Home, America," quote from pp. 5-6; see also Layne, "From Preponderance to Offshore Balancing."

17. The concept of a "legacy" grand strategy is drawn from Peter Feaver, "American Grand Strategy at the Crossroads: Leading from the Front, Leading from Behind or Not Leading at All," in Fontaine and Lord, eds., *America's Path*, esp. pp. 60-62.

18. My description of offshore balancing draws on the long bibliographic entry in Endnote 2. Where useful, it also refers to specific arguments or claims made by particular authors.

19. Quoted in Posen, "Pull Back," p. 121; see also Walt, "In the National Interest"; Walt, "End of the American Era."

20. Quotes from Christopher Layne, "The Unipolar Exit: Beyond the Pax Americana," *Cambridge Review of International Affairs*, Vol. 24, No. 2, June 2011, p. 153; Posen, "Pull Back," pp. 118, 121-123.

21. "Free-riding" (or "cheap riding) and "reckless driving" are discussed most extensively in Posen, *Restraint*, pp. 33-50.

22. Michael Birnbaum, "Gates Rebukes European Allies in Farewell Speech," *The Washington Post*, June 10, 2011.

23. Robert Pape, "Soft Balancing against the United States," *International Security*, Vol. 30, No. 1, Summer 2005, pp. 7-45.

24. See John Mearsheimer, "Why the Ukraine Crisis is the West's Fault: The Liberal Delusions That Provoked Putin," *Foreign Affairs*, Vol. 93, No. 5, September/October 2014, pp. 77-89.

25. Christopher Layne, "China's Challenge to U.S. Hegemony," *Current History*, Vol. 107, No. 705, January 2008, esp. pp. 16-18; Layne, "China's Role in American Grand Strategy: Partner, Regional Power, or Great Power Rival?" in Jim Rolfe, ed., *The Asia-Pacific: A Region of Transitions*, Honolulu, HI: The Asia-Pacific Center for Security Studies, 2004, pp. 54-80.

26. Harvey Sapolsky, Benjamin Friedman, Eugene Gholz, and Daryl Press, "Restraining Order: For Strategic Modesty," *World Affairs*, Fall 2009, esp. pp. 88-91, quoted on p. 91. For arguments regarding terrorism and proliferation, see also Pape, *Dying to Win*; Gholz and Press, "Footprints in the Sand," esp. pp. 63-65; Mearsheimer, "Imperial by Design," pp. 29-30.

27. Quoted in Colin Powell, *My American Journey*, New York: Ballantine, 1995, p. 576.

28. See, for instance, Christopher Preble, *The Power Problem: How American Military Dominance Makes Us Less Safe, Less Prosperous, and Less Free*, Ithaca, NY: Cornell University Press, 2009, esp. pp. 88-94; Posen, *Restraint*, pp. 54-60; among others.

29. These core tenets of offshore balancing can be traced in virtually any of the sources cited previously in the major bibliographic endnotes.

30. The "free-hand" concept comes from Art, *A Grand Strategy for America*, p. 172, who uses this term to categorize both offshore balancing and traditional isolationism.

31. See, as examples of these various proposals, Layne, *Peace of Illusions*; Walt, "End of the American Era"; Posen, "Pull Back"; Pape, *Dying to Win*, pp. 237-250.

32. Walt, "A Bandwagon for Offshore Balancing?"; Layne, *Peace of Illusions*, pp. 186-188; John Mearsheimer, "America Unhinged," *National Interest*, January/February 2014, esp. pp. 22-23. As Peter Feaver has written, though, one oddity of offshore balancing is that its advocates approve of such partnerships and other unsavory practices in theory, but sometimes critique them when actually undertaken. See Feaver, "Not Even One Cheer for Offshore Balancing?" *Foreign Policy*, April 30, 2013, available from *foreignpolicy.com/2013/04/30/not-even-one-cheer-for-offshore-balancing/*, accessed April 27, 2015.

33. The strongest statement of this approach is John Mearsheimer and Stephen Walt, *The Israel Lobby and U.S. Foreign Policy*, New York: Farrar, Straus, and Giroux, 2007.

34. See Layne and Schwartz, "A New Grand Strategy"; Mearsheimer, "Why the Ukraine Crisis is the West's Fault"; Layne, "China's Challenge to U.S. Hegemony," esp. pp. 17-18. As some critics of offshore balancing have noted, however, the logic of offshore balancing is not crystal clear when it comes to this issue. If offshore balancing is really all about preventing hostile powers from becoming hegemonic in key regions, then one would think that its practitioners would **not** want to concede a country like Russia or China additional influence in their regions by abandoning Taiwan or leaving Ukraine to its own devices. Rather, they might prefer to support those countries against their larger neighbors, even if only by indirect means such as arms sales or intelligence sharing, so as to raise the cost of aggression and thereby discourage future—and potentially more ambitious—efforts to upset an existing regional equilibrium.

35. See particularly Posen, *Restraint*; Mearsheimer, "Imperial by Design"; Walt, "End of the American Era."

36. John Mearsheimer, *The Tragedy of Great Power Politics*, New York: Norton, 2003, pp. 234-266. There is, however, some dispute as to whether the United States intervened in Europe in 1917 based on the logic of offshore balancing, or for other reasons. See Galen Jackson, "The Offshore Balancing Thesis Reconsidered: Realism, the Balance of Power in Europe, and America's Decision for War in 1917," *Security Studies*, Vol. 21, No. 3 August 2012, pp. 455-489. During the early-20th century, the United States did have a token military presence in East Asia, stationed in the Philippines and China.

37. After 1990, of course, the United States moved away from offshore balancing in the Gulf in favor of onshore presence. The United States similarly moved away from offshore balancing in Europe and East Asia after its victory in World War II.

38. Layne, "Offshore Balancing Revisited," pp. 245-246.

39. Posen, "Pull Back," p. 127; Preble, *Power Problem*, esp. pp. 151-156.

40. See Joshua Shifrinson and Sameer Lalwani, "It's a Common Misunderstanding: The Limited Threat to American Command of the Commons," in Christopher Preble and John Mueller, eds., *A Dangerous World? Threat Perception and U.S. National*

Security, Washington, DC: Cato Institute, 2014, esp. p. 241; also Christopher Layne, "Sleepwalking with Beijing," *National Interest*, No. 137, May/June 2015, pp. 37-45.

41. See, for instance, Mearsheimer, "Imperial by Design," p. 41.

42. Pape, *Dying to Win*, pp. 237-250, esp. pp. 237-238; Gholz and Press, "Footprints in the Sand," pp. 63-65.

43. For instance, Mearsheimer, "Imperial by Design," pp. 30, 32-33.

44. On the idea of playing hard to get, see particularly Walt, "In the National Interest." Walt is also a strong proponent of the broader idea discussed in this paragraph—that retrenchment is actually the best way to preserve American primacy and influence.

45. Preble, *Power Problem*, p. 69.

46. Precisely how much money would be saved is also difficult to say. The basic problem here is determining what one should take as the appropriate baseline. If one assumes that, in the absence of wholesale retrenchment, the United States would end up fighting Iraq- and Afghanistan-sized wars every decade, then the savings from offshore balancing would indeed be fairly substantial (although not as substantial as one might expect—see the analysis presented in the subsequent paragraph). If, however, one assumes that the better baseline would be the situation that prevailed in the 1990s (when the United States frequently used military force but generally relied on airpower in a multilateral context) or the situation that has prevailed since roughly 2011 (when the United States drew down in Iraq and began to withdraw from Afghanistan), then the savings would be much smaller still.

47. The Obama administration's FY 2015 budget request for the Defense Department, for instance, totaled over $560 billion. See Todd Harrison, *Analysis of the FY 2015 Defense Budget*, Washington, DC: Center for Strategic and Budgetary Analysis, 2014, esp. p. 5.

48. For Cold War figures, see Gaddis, *Strategies of Containment*, p. 393.

49. For post-Cold War military spending, see the data contained in World Bank, "Military Expenditure (% of GDP)," available from *data.worldbank.org/indicator/MS.MIL.XPND. GD.ZS?page=3*, accessed April 9, 2015.

50. See Amy Belasco, "The Cost of Iraq, Afghanistan, and Other Global War on Terror Operations since 9/11," Washington, DC: Congressional Research Service Report, December 2014. Data taken from "Summary."

51. For the most explicit articulation of the idea that the United States will refrain from Iraq-type conflicts in the coming years, see Department of Defense, *Sustaining U.S. Global Leadership: Priorities for 21st Century Defense*, Washington, DC: U.S. Government Printing Office, 2012, esp. pp. 3, 6.

52. Evan Braden Montgomery, "Contested Primacy in the Western Pacific: China's Rise and the Future of U.S. Power Projection," *International Security*, Vol. 38, No. 4, Spring 2014, esp. p. 121.

53. Elbridge Colby, *Grand Strategy: Contending Contemporary Analyst Views and Implications for the U.S. Navy*, Alexandria, VA: Center for Naval Analyses, November 2011, p. 29.

54. See Patrick Mills *et al.*, "The Costs of Commitment: Cost Analysis of Overseas Air Force Basing," RAND Corporation Working Paper, Santa Monica, CA: April 2012, pp. 13, 21-22. The Congressional Budget Office study is cited in the Mills paper. It is worth noting that a different RAND study takes a somewhat different view of the cost efficiencies in returning overseas forces to the United States. See Michael Lostumbo *et al.*, *Overseas Basing of U.S. Military Forces: An Assessment of Relative Costs and Strategic Benefits*, Santa Monica, CA: RAND Corporation, 2013, pp. 167-233. However, on p. 232, that study does note that "we did not find systematically higher fixed costs for overseas bases."

55. Department of Defense, *Nuclear Posture Review Report*, Washington, DC: U.S. Government Printing Office, 2010, p. 33.

56. On the importance of nuclear superiority in avoiding (and enabling) coercion, see Matthew Kroenig, "Nuclear Superiority and the Balance of Resolve: Explaining Nuclear Crisis Outcomes," *International Organization*, Vol. 67, No. 1, January 2013, pp. 141-171.

57. On the costs of nuclear modernization, see William Broad and David Sanger, "U.S. Ramping Up Major Renewal in Nuclear Arms," *The New York Times*, September 21, 2014.

58. Posen, *Restraint*, pp. 135-163, esp. p. 135.

59. See, for instance, how Posen's analysis compares to that in Holmes and Yoshihara, "An Ocean too Far," pp. 15-19.

60. On the 1999 defense budget and more recent defense spending trends, consult World Bank, "Military Expenditure (% of GDP)," available from *data.worldbank.org/indicator/MS.MIL. XPND.GD.ZS?page=3*, accessed April 9, 2015.

61. Statistics on share of federal budget available in Center on Budget and Policy Priorities, "Policy Basics: Where Do Our Federal Tax Dollars Go?" March 11, 2015, available from *www.cbpp. org/cms/?fa=view&id=1258*, accessed April 1, 2015. For recent deficits and out-year spending and deficit projections, see the various spreadsheets from Office of Management and Budget, "Historical Tables," available from *https://www.whitehouse.gov/omb/budget/ Historicals*, accessed April 1, 2015.

62. Hutchings is quoted in Dana Priest, "Iraq New Terror Breeding Ground," *The Washington Post*, January 14, 2005; also Mark Mazzetti, "Spy Agencies Say Iraq War Worsens Terrorism Threat," *The New York Times*, September 24, 2006.

63. Robert Pape and James K. Feldman, *Cutting the Fuse: The Explosion of Global Suicide Terrorism and How to Stop It*, Chicago, IL: University of Chicago Press, 2010; Pape, *Dying to Win*.

64. Daniel Byman, "A U.S. Military Withdrawal from the Greater Middle East: Impact on Terrorism," in Stephen van Evera and Sidharth Shah, *The Prudent Use of Power in American National Security Strategy*, Cambridge, MA: Tobin Project, 2010, p. 164. See

also the quote from Adam Gadahn, a now-deceased al-Qaeda spokesman, in the next paragraph.

65. World Islamic Front Statement, "Jihad Against Jews and Crusaders," February 23, 1998, available from *fas.org/irp/world/para/docs/980223-fatwa.htm*, accessed March 18, 2015; also "Bin Laden's Fatwa," PBS Newshour, August 23, 1996, available from *www.pbs.org/newshour/updates/military-july-dec96-fatwa_1996/*, accessed March 18, 2015; Byman, "A U.S. Military Withdrawal from the Greater Middle East," esp. pp. 160-162.

66. Gadahn, quoted in Robert Art, "Selective Engagement in the Era of Austerity," in Fontaine and Lord, eds., *America's Path*, p. 27.

67. See F. Gregory Gause, *The International Relations of the Persian Gulf*, New York: Cambridge University Press, 2010, p. 32.

68. Colin Kahl and Marc Lynch, "U.S. Strategy after the Arab Uprisings: Toward Progressive Engagement," *Washington Quarterly*, Vol. 36, No. 2, Summer 2013, esp. p. 52.

69. Rick Brennan, "Withdrawal Symptoms: The Bungling of the Iraq Exit," *Foreign Affairs*, Vol. 93, No. 6, November/December 2014, pp. 34-35. Indeed, it was a fear of renewed destabilization and extremism that led the Obama administration to consider leaving a residual force in Iraq after 2011, although that initiative was undone by Iraqi resistance to granting U.S. troops the legal immunity that American officials deemed necessary.

70. Art, *Grand Strategy for America*, pp. 201-202.

71. Byman, "A U.S. Military Withdrawal from the Greater Middle East," p. 157.

72. "Theory Talk #40 — Kenneth Waltz," *Theory Talks*, June 3, 2011, available from *www.theory-talks.org/2011/06/theory-talk-40.html*, accessed April 14, 2015; Nuno Monteiro, "Unrest Assured: Why Unipolarity Is Not Peaceful," *International Security*, Vol. 36, No. 3, Winter 2011/12, p. 26.

73. On Chinese motives, see M. Taylor Fravel and Evan Medeiros, "China's Search for Assured Retaliation: The Evolution of Chinese Nuclear Strategy and Force Structure," *International Security*, Vol. 35, No. 2, Fall 2010, esp. pp. 58-61.

74. The National Intelligence Council prediction can be found in National Intelligence Council, "Regional Consequences of Regime Change in Iraq," ICA-2003-03, p. 7, in Senate Select Committee on Intelligence, *Prewar Intelligence Assessments about Postwar Iraq*, Washington, DC: U.S. Government Printing Office, 2007.

75. On the range of motives that can inform proliferation, see Scott D. Sagan, "Why Do States Build Nuclear Weapons? Three Models in Search of a Bomb," *International Security*, Vol. 21, No. 3, Winter 1996/97, pp. 54-86.

76. Hal Brands and David Palkki, "Saddam, Israel, and the Bomb: Nuclear Alarmism Justified?" *International Security*, Vol. 36, No. 1, Summer 2011, pp. 133-166, quoted on p. 133.

77. Department of Defense, *Nuclear Posture Review Report*, p. xii. This page of the report also notes that such arrangements limit proliferation by demonstrating to non-allies "that their pursuit of nuclear weapons will only undermine their goal of achieving military or political advantages."

78. Gene Gerzhoy, "Alliance Coercion and Nuclear Restraint: How the United States Thwarted West Germany's Nuclear Ambitions," *International Security*, Vol. 39, No. 4, Spring 2015, pp. 91-129.

79. Miller, "Hegemony and Nuclear Proliferation."

80. See Gerzhoy, "Alliance Coercion and Nuclear Restraint"; the cases discussed in Gavin, "Strategies of Inhibition," pp. 26-28 (page numbers from unpublished manuscript); also Bruno Tertrais, "Security Guarantees and Nuclear Non-Proliferation," Paris, France: *Fondation pour la Recherche Strategique* (Foundation for Strategic Research), Note 14/11, 2011, available from *https://www.frstrategie.org/barreFRS/publications/notes/2011/201114.pdf*, accessed March 26, 2015.

81. See John Mearsheimer, "Back to the Future: Instability in Europe after the Cold War," *International Security*, Vol. 15, No. 1, Summer 1990, pp. 5-56.

82. See Mark Kramer, "Neorealism, Nuclear Proliferation, and East-Central European Strategies," in Ethan Kapstein and Michael Mastanduno, eds., *Unipolar Politics: Realism and State Strategies after the Cold War*, New York: Columbia University Press, 1999, pp. 385-463.

83. Gavin, "Strategies of Inhibition," p. 26 (page number taken from unpublished manuscript). See also Robert Einhorn, "Ukraine, Security Assurances, and Nonproliferation," *Washington Quarterly*, Vol. 38, No. 1, Spring 2015, esp. pp. 52-54.

84. As Toshi Yoshihara and James Holmes argue, for instance, a major drop-off in U.S. forward presence in East Asia could have:

> major diplomatic ramifications—it would undercut America's staying power in the western Pacific, give rise to Japanese fears of abandonment, and unsettle the entire Asian security architecture. More to the point, Tokyo would likely interpret such a decline as foreshadowing an end to the U.S. nuclear guarantee.

See Holmes and Yoshihara, "Thinking about the Unthinkable: Tokyo's Nuclear Option," in Holmes and Yoshihara, eds., *Strategy in the Second Nuclear Age: Power, Ambition, and the Ultimate Weapon*, Washington, DC: Georgetown University Press, 2012, p. 116.

85. These dynamics can be seen in David Sanger, "Saudi Arabia Promises to Match Iran in Nuclear Capability," *The New York Times*, May 13, 2015. Similarly, as three expert observers noted in an earlier report:

> U.S. conventional forces deployed in the frontline states of the Persian Gulf would play an especially important role in reinforcing extended deterrence, containing the prospect of emboldened Iranian conventional or irregular aggression and reassuring anxious regional allies and partners.

Colin Kahl, Raj Pattani, and Jacob Stokes, *If All Else Fails: The Challenges of Containing a Nuclear-Armed Iran,* Washington, DC: Center for a New American Security, 2013, p. 36.

86. Offshore balancers have occasionally discounted this prospect by arguing that the United States could mitigate proliferation, even following retrenchment, by simply stating that countries in East Asia, the Persian Gulf, and Europe remained under the U.S. "nuclear umbrella" — in essence, that Washington would still defend them from attack by a nuclear-armed aggressor. (See Mearsheimer, "Imperial by Design," p. 32.) Yet this assertion is dubious. Leaving aside the fact that this approach would leave the United States saddled with precisely the security guarantees to which offshore balances often object, this argument misses the fact that forward presence is so frequently what makes security commitments credible. During the Cold War, for example, it was one thing to **say** that the United States was committed to the defense of West Germany. It was another thing entirely to station U.S. troops in West Germany to ensure that any attack on West Germany would be an attack on American forces as well. In other words, reassurance is as much a function of presence as of declared intent — indeed, the former makes the latter believable.

87. These arguments draw on the founding statement of "proliferation optimism," Kenneth Waltz's "The Spread of Nuclear Weapons: More May Be Better," *Adelphi Papers,* No. 171, London, UK: International Institute for Strategic Studies, 1981.

88. The danger of nuclear terrorism is discussed in Graham Allison, *Nuclear Terrorism: The Ultimate Preventable Catastrophe,* New York: Macmillan, 2004.

89. See Peter Feaver, "Command and Control in Emerging Nuclear Nations," *International Security,* Vol. 17, No. 3, Winter 1992/93, pp. 160-187; also the contributions by Peter Feaver, Scott Sagan, and David J. Karl, "Proliferation Pessimism and Emerging Nuclear Powers," *International Security,* Vol. 22, No. 2, Fall 1997, pp. 185-207.

90. See Robert Rachhaus, "Evaluating the Nuclear Peace Hypothesis: A Quantitative Approach," *Journal of Conflict Resolution,* Vol. 53, No. 2, April 2009, pp. 258-277; S. Paul Kapur, "Ten Years of Instability in a Nuclear South Asia," *International Security,* Vol.

33, No. 2, Fall 2008, pp. 45-70; and Michael Horowitz, "The Spread of Nuclear Weapons and International Conflict: Does Experience Matter?" *Journal of Conflict Resolution*, Vol. 53, No. 2, April 2009, pp. 234-257.

91. A thorough analysis of the impact of the Iraq War on U.S. soft power is Ole Holsti, *To See Ourselves as Others See Us: How Publics Abroad View the United States after 9/11*, Ann Arbor, MI: University of Michigan Press, 2008.

92. The best critique is Stephen Brooks and William Wohlforth, "Hard Times for Soft Balancing," *International Security*, Vol. 30, No. 1, Summer 2005, pp. 72-108; also Keir Lieber and Gerard Alexander, "Waiting for Balancing: Why the World is Not Pushing Back," *International Security*, Vol. 30, No. 1, Summer 2005, pp. 109-139.

93. The best analysis is Zachary Selden, "Balancing Against or Balancing With? The Spectrum of Alignment and the Endurance of American Hegemony," *Security Studies*, Vol. 22, No. 3, May 2013, pp. 330-363. See also Michael Green, "The Iraq War and Asia: Assessing the Legacy," *Washington Quarterly*, Vol. 31, No. 2, Spring 2008, pp. 181-200.

94. See the analysis in Jordan Becker, "Offshore Balancing or Overbalancing? A Preliminary Empirical Analysis of the Effect of U.S. Troop Presence on the Political Behavior of Regional Partners," in Joseph da Silva, Hugh Liebert, and Isaiah Wilson III., eds., *American Grand Strategy and the Future of Landpower*, Carlisle, PA: Strategic Studies Institute, U.S. Army War College, 2014, pp. 261-286, quoted on p. 263; also Nigel Thalakada, *Unipolarity and the Evolution of America's Cold War Alliances*, New York: Palgrave Macmillan, 2012, esp. pp. 12-13, 17-19.

95. This leverage could even be invoked in dealing with major allies. In 1963, for example, Washington employed the influence generated by its security presence to help push Konrad Adenauer out of office after he sought to realign West German policy in ways unfavorable to the United States. On this episode, see Marc Trachtenberg, *A Constructed Peace: The Making of the European Settlement, 1945-1963*, Princeton, NJ: Princeton University Press, 1999, pp. 370-379.

96. On the intersection between U.S. presence and the dollar, see Francis Gavin, *Gold, Dollars, and Power: The Politics of International Monetary Relations, 1958-1971,* Chapel Hill, NC: University of North Carolina Press, 2004, esp. pp. 30-31, 113-114, 165-166. On the U.S.-South Korea negotiations, see Brooks, Ikenberry, and Wohlforth, "Don't Come Home, America," pp. 43-44.

97. Mearsheimer, "Why is Europe Peaceful Today?" *European Political Science,* Vol. 9, No. 2, September 2010, esp. p. 388. Mearsheimer is talking here about the post-Cold War period specifically, but the argument applies equally to the Cold War era. For an account of how U.S. power played a stabilizing role (and how U.S. efforts to withdraw could be intensely destabilizing) during the early decades of the Cold War, see Trachtenberg, *Constructed Peace.*

98. Mandelbaum, *Case for Goliath,* pp. 31-87, esp. p. 35.

99. The importance of interoperability and training is emphasized in John Deni, *The Future of American Landpower: Does Forward Presence Still Matter? The Case of the Army in Europe,* Carlisle, PA: Strategic Studies Institute, U.S. Army War College, 2012; also Deni, *The Future of American Landpower: Does Forward Presence Still Matter? The Case of the Army in the Pacific,* Carlisle, PA: Strategic Studies Institute, U.S. Army War College, 2014.

100. As noted, however, it is not assured that withdrawal would indeed compel local or regional powers to provide more effectively for their own defense (at least on terms that would be favorable to the United States). If a U.S. withdrawal left local actors with little hope of effectively resisting a larger, expansionist neighbor, they might choose to acquiesce to that neighbor instead.

101. Mearsheimer, "Why is Europe Peaceful Today?" p. 389. In fact, Mearsheimer himself has long predicted that increased instability would follow U.S. retreat from key geopolitical areas. See Mearsheimer, "Back to the Future."

102. For a good recent analysis, see Stephen Larrabee, Peter Wilson, and John Gordon IV, *The Ukrainian Crisis and European Security: Implications for the United States and U.S. Army,* Santa Monica, CA: RAND Corporation, 2015.

103. For the early post-Cold War analysis, see Aaron L. Fried-berg, "Ripe for Rivalry: Prospects for Peace in a Multipolar Asia," *International Security*, Vol. 18, No. 3, Winter 1993/94, pp. 5-33. On Asia particularly, see also the essays in Thomas Mahnken and Dan Blumenthal, *Strategy in Asia: The Past, Present, and Future of Regional Security*, Stanford, CA: Stanford University Press, 2014. For a good analysis tying many of the recent regional trends to-gether, see Walter Russell Mead, "The Return of Geopolitics: The Revenge of the Revisionist Powers," *Foreign Affairs*, Vol. 93, No. 3, May/June 2014, pp. 69-79.

104. Christopher Layne, for one, has contended that more in-tense regional security competitions in key regions would actual-ly benefit Washington by absorbing the energies of countries that might otherwise challenge it for international primacy. He writes:

> As an offshore balancer, the United States could maximize its relative power effortlessly by standing on the sidelines while other great powers enervate themselves in security competitions with one another.

Layne, *Peace of Illusions*, p. 161.

105. See, for instance, Smith, *America's Mission*, pp. 146-176; Ikenberry, *After Victory*, esp. pp. 236-239; John Lewis Gaddis, *We Now Know: Rethinking Cold War History*, New York: Oxford University Press, 1997, pp. 198-200.

106. Art, *Grand Strategy for America*, p. 221. See also Richard Rosecrance, "Shaping Strategies: Geopolitics and the U.S. Army," in da Silva, Liebert, and Wilson, eds., *American Grand Strategy and the Future of U.S. Landpower*, pp. 256-257.

107. As Tony Smith notes, the impact of those initiatives has indeed been quite significant. Smith, *America's Mission*.

108. See Mandelbaum, *Case for Goliath*, pp. 88-140.

109. This point is mentioned in Thomas Christensen, "Foster-ing Stability or Creating a Monster? The Rise of China and U.S. Policy toward East Asia," *International Security*, Vol. 31, No. 1, Summer 2006, esp. p. 106.

110. On the concept of underbalancing, see Randall Schweller, *Unanswered Threats: Political Constraints on the Balance of Power*, Princeton, NJ: Princeton University Press, 2006.

111. As Ernest May has argued, in fact, the French and the British actually had a number of significant advantages over the Germans in early-1940, which made their subsequent collapse all the more startling. See Ernest May, *Strange Victory: Hitler's Conquest of France*, New York: Farrar, Straus & Giroux, 2000. Similarly, at the outset of the Pacific War, Japan conquered vast swaths of the Asia-Pacific in far less time and with far less difficulty than most observers had expected.

112. As one U.S. military official later recalled:

Quite frankly, we could not have issued speeding tickets to the tanks as they would have come rolling down the interstate highway on the east coast. It was an opportunity the Iraqis did not take.

Quoted in Frederick Kagan, *Finding the Target: The Transformation of American Military Policy*, New York: Encounter Books, 2007, p. 133. Similarly, President George H.W. Bush later offered a similar assessment: if Saddam had moved into Saudi Arabia promptly, "he would have had a free run." See George Bush and Brent Scowcroft, *A World Transformed*, New York: Vintage, 1999, p. 335.

113. A good assessment of the limitations of Chinese capabilities is Michael Chase *et al.*, *China's Incomplete Military Transformation: Assessing the Weaknesses of the People's Liberation Army (PLA)*, Santa Monica, CA: RAND Corporation, 2015.

114. Mearsheimer, "Imperial by Design," p. 33. On the rise of Chinese power and its implications for East Asia, see also Thomas Mahnken *et al.*, *Asia in the Balance: Transforming U.S. Military Strategy in Asia*, Washington, DC: American Enterprise Institute, 2012, esp. pp. 9-12; Aaron Friedberg, *A Contest for Supremacy: China, America, and the Struggle for Mastery in Asia*, New York: Norton, 2011; Michael Swaine *et al.*, *China's Military and the U.S.-Japan Alliance in 2030: A Strategic Net Assessment*, Washington, DC: Carnegie Endowment for International Peace, 2013.

115. Robert Gilpin, *War and Change in World Politics*, New York: Cambridge University Press, 1983, p. 194. For a contemporary application of this insight, see Colin Dueck, *The Obama Doctrine: American Grand Strategy Today*, New York: Oxford University Press, 2015.

116. Quoted in Seth Mydans, "Vietnam Finds an Old Foe Has New Allure," *The New York Times*, April 13, 2000. See also Selden, "Balancing Against or Balancing With?" esp. pp. 338-339.

117. Selden, "Balancing Against or Balancing With?" esp. pp. 331, 338-339. The Thai observer is also quoted here.

118. In fairness to offshore balancers, it might be objected that not all of the pernicious consequences of offshore balancing can materialize at the same time. If U.S. retrenchment leads to widespread nuclear proliferation in East Asia, for instance, then that would presumably indicate that underbalancing was not occurring, and that China might have more difficulty asserting primacy in the region. For the sake of argument, assume that this objection is warranted and that these two scenarios—underbalancing and proliferation—are mutually exclusive. Either way, the probable outcome of offshore balancing would still be worse than the situation that prevails today. Instead of a relatively underproliferated East Asia in which U.S. presence fortifies local actors against a rising China, the United States would face either: a) a more proliferated and dangerous region; or b) an underproliferated region that might have less confidence in facing a rising China. Neither option is desirable from a U.S. perspective; the only question is which would be worse.

119. According to many accounts, U.S. intervention in the Taiwan Strait crisis of 1995-96 was a crucial turning point, convincing Beijing that it needed far greater military capabilities if it were to prevent future U.S. meddling in the Taiwan issue. On that episode, see Robert Suettinger, *Beyond Tiananmen: The Politics of U.S.-China Relations, 1989-2000*, Washington, DC: Brookings Institution Press, 2003, pp. 246-263.

120. This point is made by Christensen, "Fostering Stability or Creating a Monster?" esp. pp. 116-119.

121. Friedberg, *A Contest for Supremacy*, p. 254, raises a similar concern about U.S. retrenchment in the face of a rising China.

122. As discussed earlier, the argument that offshore balancing would allow the United States to increase its focus on East Asia is also undercut by the fact that the strategy would likely encourage increased instability and conflict in other key regions, thereby harming important American interests in the process.

123. Holmes and Yoshihara, "An Ocean Too Far," p. 11.

124. Art, *A Grand Strategy for America*, p. 205. On the value of forward presence in the Pacific, see also Deni, *The Future of American Landpower: Does Forward Presence Still Matter? The Case of the Army in the Pacific.*

125. One question that is sometimes raised with respect to U.S.-China relations and the future of East Asia is why the United States could not simply tolerate Chinese primacy in that region, just as Great Britain actually strengthened its faltering global position by acceding to U.S. primacy in the Western Hemisphere beginning in the 1890s. This analogy, unfortunately, is flawed on at least two grounds. First, for Great Britain, it made strategic sense to appease the United States because London faced another rising enemy that posed a far greater long-term threat to its security — Germany. In the current situation, by contrast, there is no greater threat — China itself poses the biggest long-term danger to American primacy. Second, Britain could more easily tolerate growing U.S. influence because both countries were democratic states that possessed roughly compatible views of world order. With respect to the United States and China today, there is greater reason to doubt whether such compatibility exists.

126. Holmes and Yoshihara, "An Ocean Too Far," p. 1; also Francis Fukuyama, "Dealing with ISIS: Offshore Balancing in the Middle East," *The American Interest*, March 23, 2015, available from *www.the-american-interest.com/2015/03/23/dealing-with-isis/*, accessed May 14, 2015; Mearsheimer, "A Return to Offshore Balancing," *Newsweek*, December 30, 2008, available from *www.newsweek.com/return-offshore-balancing-82925*, accessed April 14, 2015.

127. See Brooks, Ikenberry, and Wohlforth, "Don't Come Home, America"; Michael Beckley, "The Myth of Entangling Alliances: Reassessing the Security Risks of U.S. Defense Pacts," *International Security*, Vol. 39, No. 4, Spring 2015, pp. 7-48; Beckley, "China's Century? Why America's Edge Will Endure," *International Security*, Vol. 36, No. 3, Winter 2011/12, pp. 41-78.

128. The point is also made by Robert Kagan, "The Price of Power," *Weekly Standard*, January 24, 2011, available from *www.weeklystandard.com/articles/price-power_533695.html#*, accessed May 18, 2015.

129. For one such proposal, see Posen, "Pull Back," p. 127. See also Gary Roughead and Kori Schake, "National Defense in a Time of Change," Hamilton Project Discussion Paper Brief 2013-01, February 2013, p. 13, available from *www.ngaus.org/sites/default/files/HamiltonProjectBrookingsRougheadPaper2013.pdf*, accessed June 2, 2015.

130. Quote from U.S. Army, U.S. Marine Corps, and U.S. Special Operations Command, *Strategic Landpower: Winning the Clash of Wills*, October 2013, available from *www.arcic.army.mil/app_Documents/Strategic-Landpower-White-Paper-28OCT2013.pdf*, accessed June 2, 2015. On the enduring importance of Landpower, see also Deni, *The Future of American Landpower*, 2012 and 2014; Nathan Freier *et al*, *Beyond the Last War: Balancing Ground Forces and Future Challenges Risk in USCENTCOM and USPACOM*, Washington, DC: Center for Strategic and International Studies, 2013; and Steven Metz, *Strategic Landpower Task Force Research Report*, October 2013, available from *www.strategicstudiesinstitute.army.mil/index.cfm/articles/STRATEGIC-LANDPOWER-TASK-FORCE/2013/10/3*, accessed June 2, 2015.

131. See Hal Brands, *What Good is Grand Strategy? Power and Purpose in American Statecraft from Harry S. Truman to George W. Bush*, Ithaca, NY: Cornell University Press, 2014.

132. Gaddis, *Strategies of Containment*; Brooks, Ikenberry, and Wohlforth, "Don't Come Home, America," pp. 12-13, 32-33, 50-51.

133. On Eisenhower, see Robert Bowie and Richard Immerman, *Waging Peace: How Eisenhower Shaped an Enduring Cold War*

Strategy, New York: Oxford University Press, 1998; on Nixon, see Gaddis, *Strategies of Containment*, Chaps. 9-10.

134. For an assessment stressing both positive and negative aspects of this recalibration, see Hal Brands, "Breaking Down Obama's Grand Strategy," *National Interest*, June 23, 2014, available from *nationalinterest.org/feature/breaking-down-obamas-grand-strategy-10719*, accessed May 12, 2015.

135. See Bruce Jentleson, "Strategic Recalibration: Framework for a 21st-Century National Security Strategy," *Washington Quarterly*, Vol. 37, No. 1, Spring 2014, pp. 115-136; Feaver, "American Grand Strategy at the Crossroads"; Art, "Selective Engagement in the Era of Austerity."

U.S. ARMY WAR COLLEGE

Major General William E. Rapp
Commandant

*****

STRATEGIC STUDIES INSTITUTE
and
U.S. ARMY WAR COLLEGE PRESS

Director
Professor Douglas C. Lovelace, Jr.

Director of Research
Dr. Steven K. Metz

Author
Dr. Hal Brands

Editor for Production
Dr. James G. Pierce

Publications Assistant
Ms. Rita A. Rummel

*****

Composition
Mrs. Jennifer E. Nevil

CPSIA information can be obtained at www.ICGtesting.com
Printed in the USA
BVOW08s1249080916

461436BV00037B/37/P